'These Uncertaine Tymes'

Newark and the Civilian Experience of the Civil Wars 1640-1660

Stuart B. Jennings

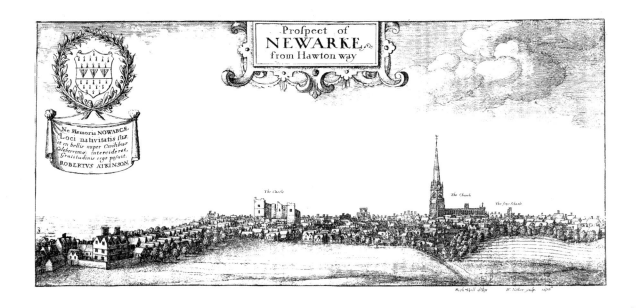

Nottinghamshire
County Council

Stuart Jennings studied for an MA in Local and Regional History at the University of Nottingham and went on to complete a doctorate in History at Nottingham Trent University. He is a chaplain to the University of Warwick and Coventry University and also academic co-ordinator and lecturer in Local History at the University of Warwick Centre for Life-long Learning. He has published numerous articles and essays on the British Civil Wars.

Acknowledgements

The author would like to record his thanks to the following individuals. Professor Martyn Bennett, my colleague and friend, whose support and advice helped bring this book to completion and for his additional generosity in writing the preface. Also to Mark Dorrington (Principal Archivist) and Tim Warner (Local Studies Librarian) with Nottinghamshire County Council who proof read the text and offered much constructive advice, and Jo Peet at the Nottinghamshire Archives who guided me through the Newark Corporation papers at a time when they were not fully catalogued. Also to Gillian Elias for permission to use her drawing of the Queen's Sconce, and to Sharon Ingham for her illuminating notes on Richard Clampe's plan. Newark & Sherwood District Council Museums kindly allowed some of their collection of Civil War artefacts to be photographed especially for this publication by photographer Jon Higgins. Finally my thanks go to the editor of *Midland History* who first published some of the research contained in Chapter 4 in a paper of the same title. This book is dedicated to my wife Carol who has patiently endured my ongoing research into seventeenth century Newark for several years.

Copyright: Stuart Jennings 2009

ISBN: 978-0-902751-62-0

Printed and designed by: Nottinghamshire County Council, Design, Publications and Print, 2009

Front Cover illustration: The gatehouse at Newark Castle

Title Page illustration: 'Prospect of Newark from Hawton Way' by Richard Hall, 1676 (From Robert Thoroton's *Antiquities of Nottinghamshire* (1677)

CONTENTS

List of Plates   ii

List of Tables   ii

Maps   ii

Preface   iii

Introduction   1

1.   *'A very neate...built town'*:
Newark in the early seventeenth century   6

2.   *'The warre between the king and parliament'*:
Newark 1642-1646   18

3.   *'The miseries and affliccions of these tymes'*:
Debt, dearth and destruction; the
civilian experience of war 1642-1648   37

4.   *'A miserable, stinking, infected town'*:
Pestilence, plague and death, 1640-1649   62

5.   *'What is the city but the people?'*:
Marriage, childbirth, commerce and community
in a time of war and disruption   85

6.   *'The people of England...shall henceforth be
governed as a Commonwealth and free state'*:
Newark in the 1650s   97

7.   *'Ad majorem Dei Gloriam'*
The life and worship of the parish church
1640-1660   108

Epilogue   125

End Notes   128

Bibliography   135

List of Plates (Between pages 84-85)

1. Newark Castle; the west curtain wall
2. Newark Castle; gatehouse and north-west tower
3. Newark Castle; 12th century gatehouse
4. Newark Castle; Middle Tower in the west curtain wall
5. The parish church of St.Mary Magdalene, Newark-on-Trent
6. The spire of the parish church of St.Mary Magdalene
7. Newark Market Place; the Olde White Hart Inn
8. Pamphlet recording the speech delivered to the Trained Bands
9. Prince Rupert
10. The Governor's House, Stodman Street, Newark
11. Detail from Richard Clampe's plan of the Third Siege of Newark
12. A Newark Siege Coin
13. An artist's impression of the Queen's Sconce during the Third Siege
14, 15 & 16.   A selection of Civil War artefacts found around Newark

List of Tables

1.1	Charitable endowments in use during the seventeenth century	14
3.1	Loans made to the Royalist cause	40
4.1	Pre-civil war mortality figures for Newark	64
4.2	Annual burial data used for table 4.1	64
4.3	Burials 1642-1648	67
4.4	Baptisms and burials, 1642-1648	68
5.1	Marriages at Newark, 1631-1660	88
5.2	Poor relief details 1639-40 and 1645-46	90
5.3	Masters of the Newark Grammar School, 1642-1660	95
6.1	Individuals who supported the king but continued to serve in office after the surrender of the town in 1646	100
6.2	Burials and baptisms, 1650-1660	104
7.1	Churchwarden account details 1640-1660	110

Map

Newark and its surroundings at the time of the third siege, 1646   71

PREFACE

Nottinghamshire has the reputation as the county where the first Civil War began. On 22 August 1642 King Charles I and his embryonic army returned to Nottingham, after an expedition to Coventry, to raise the royal standard in the precincts of the town's venerable castle. The king's action is taken as the starting date for the war and seen as the point at which the fighting began. This view is not quite correct however, as fighting had occurred before the 22 August and political negotiations continued afterwards, but the act could be seen as the symbolic declaration of the king's war on the Westminster Parliament. Historians in the late twentieth century also saw the event as symbolic of the lack of popular support for the king. Very few soldiers were present when the standard was first flown and this was interpreted as showing a lack of support for the Royalist cause. However, the king had troops scattered between Warwickshire and Nottinghamshire, some making their way back towards Nottingham after the failed attempts to grab the Warwickshire magazine stored in Coventry. The 300 soldiers present came from the Nottinghamshire trained bands, the county's militia, and truly represented the hard work of the county's constables who had roused their village's soldiers and packed them off to Nottingham on hired horses at very short notice.

If anywhere in the county could be considered symbolic of the war it may instead be Newark, where on 5 May 1646 the king handed himself over to his Scottish enemies and ordered the Royalist garrison to surrender. If anything represents the support for the Royalist cause, it is the fact the after six months of being besieged the town and garrison had no plans to surrender, and when he did hand over his charge, the governor John Lord Bellasyse had tears in his eyes.

Newark was an important market town in the region, not only for Nottinghamshire, but also for adjacent Lincolnshire. The town was situated on two important communications routes: it was on the banks of the river Trent which brought trade not only from the west and north, but also from the continent because of its link to the Humber estuary: Newark also bestrode the Great North Road stretching from London to York and beyond, which allowed the town to export produce from its markets up and down the country. Unfortunately, as in any war, the very things that sustain and develop a community and its economy are also strategically important, and this made Newark a target for both sides during the Civil War. The river Trent was quickly neutralised: Parliamentarian possession of Hull closed one end of the route to Royalists and the garrison at Nottingham prevented Royalists using the westward route; likewise the Royalist garrison at Newark limited the river's value to Parliamentarians. The Great North Road was of greater value allowing Royalists to move northward quickly. The road was a target for East Anglian Parliamentarians, sometimes under Oliver Cromwell, who sought to control access between London and the north.

Forces under Scottish professional soldier Sir John Henderson garrisoned Newark shortly before Christmas 1642, although it had been the site of Royalist meetings held by High Sheriff Sir John Digby from November onwards. Nottingham had also been garrisoned, but this time by Parliamentarians led by Sir John Hutchinson. Thus the south of the county was polarised, for whilst both sides established satellite garrisons, the two chief towns – Nottingham and Newark - remained in opposing hands until Newark was ordered to surrender on 5 May 1646.

Dr Jennings's book focuses on Newark's survival during the war; the town's war record has attracted historians' interests previously: in the nineteenth century Cornelius Brown dealt with the war in two books. In the 1930s Professor Alfred Wood wrote his classic history of the Civil War in Nottinghamshire and in the 1960s the Royal Commission on Historical Monuments produced its important survey on the Civil War siegeworks in and around the town. Almost 30 years later Tim Warner produced an excellent brief digest of the siegeworks as part of the commemoration of the opening of the Civil Wars in England and Wales 350 years earlier. Dr Jennings has created this history from the sources available to past historians but also by using sources newly released into the public domain. The council papers of the borough, through which Dr Jennings has acted as an unguided explorer and cataloguer have enabled the creation of a unique view of Newark in the Civil War. The town underwent three sieges, February 1643, February – March 1644 and finally November 1645 to May 1646, each increasing in duration and intensity. There is no doubting the appalling nature of these events, as the memoirs of townsman John Twentyman make clear. However, they were only part of the picture. Newark was a garrison for three and half years with over two thousand soldiers continuously based there, stabling their horses and eating, drinking, living and dying in the market town. Dr Jennings's book looks not only at the frightening emergencies imposed by the three sieges, but also the mundane acts of garrison life such as cleaning the stables occupied by the garrison's horses. The town underwent a series of changes during the war; its appearance was altered by the destruction and demolition of buildings because of construction work and enemy action. The construction of defence works changed the look of the town. An ever increasing series of earthworks was built around the town in response to the sieges of 1643 and 1644. This is the town's Civil War legacy as conditions after the war prevented the dismantling of the defence works; they are also the town's legacy to history for they remain to be explored by historians on a scale unrivalled anywhere else. The book looks at the war and how the town and its people survived rebuilding their economy afterwards in difficult circumstances. Trade was destroyed by the final six month siege and disease spread throughout the surrounding communities. Dr Jennings traces the considerable time and effort needed to reconstruct the economic life of the town. He goes on to look at the way the town experienced the second Civil War and the establishment of the Republic. Dr Jennings reveals how, for Newark, the Republic was unproblematic - a view that coincides with current research which suggests that had it not imploded at the centre, the Republic could have thrived at local and regional level.

Stuart Jennings is a graduate of both of Nottingham's universities and is well placed to write this history. His research on the Parkyns family of Bunny in the seventeenth century at Nottingham University brought him into contact with Royalist Colonel Isham Parkyns. During his PhD research at Nottingham Trent University Stuart published work on the account book of the Newark based regiment of Colonel William Staunton. This latter acted as a springboard for this book. Stuart Jennings's work gives a rounded perspective of a town's survival in the Civil War and thus complements the work of Stephen Porter's *London and the Civil War* (London, 1996), Malcolm Atkin and M. Laughton's *Gloucester in the Civil War* (Stroud, 1992), Peter Wenham's *Great and Close Siege of York* (Kineton, 1970), and John Wroughton's *A Community at War: The Civil War in Bath and North Somerset* (Bath, 1992). Each of these works adds to the pointillism of civil war history, and reveals something of the exigencies of war and survival in urban communities. This is true also of Dr Jennings's work on Newark, which demonstrates the resilience of the local community in the face of war and revolution - the 'uncertaine tymes' at the heart of the seventeenth century.

Martyn Bennett
Nottingham Trent University

INTRODUCTION

From the moment that fighting ceased in May 1646 Newark's military role during the first Civil War was a matter of debate, and in some quarter's pride. As early as 1654 the diarist John Evelyn was referring to Newark as that 'brave Towne and Garrison'[1], whilst just over fifty years later the author Daniel Defoe wrote a much fuller praise of the town during his tour around the country.

> At Newark one can hardly see without regret the ruins of that famous castle, which maintained itself through the whole civil war in England, and keeping a strong garrison there for the king, cut off the greatest pass in the north that is in the whole kingdom; nor was it taken, 'till the king, pressed by the calamity of his affairs, put himself into the hands of the Scots army, which lay before it, and then commanded the governor to deliver it up, after which it was demolished, that the great road might lie open and free.[2]

Enduring three sieges, the last of which was imposed by both English and Scottish armies, entertaining the king and his army on several occasions and also Prince Rupert and Queen Henrietta and their armies, evidence of the town's Royalism is writ large in the ruins of its castle and in the surrounding fields. To this day Newark still possess some of the finest surviving civil war siegeworks anywhere in the country.[3]

Between 1642 and 1660, Newark was not simply a garrison of soldiers but also a town of over 2,000 citizens who sought to maintain their daily regime of earning a living, raising a family and creating a home. To them the momentous events unfolding all around were probably viewed with a mixture of bewilderment, anguish and grim resignation. These people were the silent witnesses to the war, often over-looked or misrepresented because their experiences were rarely recorded and, if they were, they have failed to survive. The town's stubborn resistance and resilience, maintaining an unconquered garrison throughout the course of the war, may have created considerable hardship for its citizens but it has had one unexpected and surprising consequence for subsequent historians (though rarely used until now). Many of the ordinary records of day-to-day life have not only survived until the present day but were reasonably well maintained throughout the war. These are far from comprehensive or complete, but they do testify to a continuity of civic life under the military regime and provide an invaluable snapshot of civilian life in Newark often missing from other towns of the period. Recently deposited records at the local archives include Newark Borough minutes and miscellaneous papers, fragmentary poor relief accounts, churchwarden's accounts and even a set of military accounts for one of the regiments based at the town.[4] Such information is not only a resource for the local historian but also for those who seek to construct a wider picture of the social consequences of the Civil War. It is this previously unused material that forms the basis of the book that follows.

In 1600 Newark upon Trent was the second largest town in the county of Nottingham. Situated alongside a secondary arm of the river Trent, it provided the only crossing point over the river before it reached the Humber estuary. The town also lay astride the Great North Road which linked the capital with York and Newcastle. Through the town itself, meanwhile, ran the old Roman Fosse Way, which traversed the country from east to west. Newark's situation on these major transportation routes, both road and river, made it an important centre for trade and commerce. A market was held every Wednesday, which particularly dealt with cattle, and there were four great annual fairs, which attracted large crowds into the town. In May of every year virtually the whole town journeyed to nearby Coddington Moor to see the annual horse race and fair organised by the borough council.

The first chapter of this book provides an analysis of everyday life in Newark over the first four decades of the seventeenth century. It explores the town's administrative and economic structures and the way in which the town and its citizens reacted to unfolding national politics, the developing religious policy of Archbishop Laud and imposition of new taxes after 1629. The town community was in many ways very traditional in its outlook and both ship money and the enforcement of alterations to the parish church were not generally well received. In fact there is nothing in these four decades that foreshadows Newark's future Royalist allegiance. In many ways the town was a typical representation of many English urban communities during this period.

It is now over forty years since a last major review and history of Newark's military involvement in the Civil War was written.[5]   Therefore in order to be able to set social and economic developments in their proper context, the book provides a new narrative account of the military events that took place around Newark. Contemporary eyewitness accounts, such as that of Newark citizen John Twentyman, and newly published research, all contribute to a fresh understanding of the effects of military events as they unfolded.   Chapters three and four will provide an in-depth analysis of the consequences of the war for the civilians of the town.   Issues such as the destruction of property, taxation, billeting of soldiers, trade and the administration of the town are all examined and assessed for their impact upon the inhabitants of Newark.   The demographic consequences of the war for civilian populations have long been acknowledged and chapter four provides a detailed survey of the situation in Newark.   As this research will clearly demonstrate, typhus the common disease of field armies, and later plague were to kill up to 25 per cent of the civilian population in a four year period.   It would take a number of decades before the population of the town was restored to its pre-war size of around 2,300 persons.

Despite the disruptions caused by the war over the years 1642-1646, the 'natural rulers' of the town exerted considerable energies in maintaining the daily routine of everyday life.   Levies continued to be raised and poor relief administered so that the most vulnerable did not starve.   Those periods when the town was besieged meant that there were times when rents from the surrounding borough lands could not be collected, especially from November 1645 through to Newark's surrender in May 1646. This resulted in the amount of cash available for charitable purposes being much reduced.   Yet as chapter five will demonstrate, the town authorities were able to maintain a degree of order.   Civic offices were filled, markets held and marriage and the raising of families continued.   The degree of continuity in the face of adversity was a testimony to the resilience of the local population and also of local government.

The ending of the war did not bring an immediate resolution of the difficulties. Nationally the political scene lurched from crisis to crisis culminating in the execution of Charles I in 1649 and the establishment of a Commonwealth and later a Protectorate.[6]   Those who had been loyal to the Royalist cause - and there were many in Newark - often found themselves excluded from government and subject to many financial and social penalties.   Throughout the 1650s national developments began to percolate down to local communities.   Chapter five explores how Newark experienced and responded to being part of a new republican regime. What seems to emerge - at least in the case of Newark - is a triumph of localism over the centre, though not without some restrictions.   During the latter part of the 1650s the nation experienced a deteriorating economic situation and a succession of poor or inadequate harvests.   The chapter ends by exploring the consequences of this for the citizens of the town.

In the seventeenth century, religion lay at the heart of political, social and everyday life.   At the start of the Civil War in 1642 there existed a single national church to which everyone belonged, centred on the liturgy contained in the *Book of Common Prayer*.   Magistrate and ministry were the focus of good government and social order.   Once fighting had ceased, this national ecclesiastical consensus was shattered, episcopacy was abolished and the Prayer Book prohibited.   In their place came assemblies of like-minded believers and a new *Directory of Worship*, loosely modelled on the Presbyterian form of church government.   To many, this seemed to result in an anarchy of religious expression that threatened the very order of society itself.   In the final chapter this book seeks to explore how this developing religious scene was experienced in Newark where, in spite of the presence of Parliamentarian troops for much of the 1650s and the ejection of their own minister at the start of the 1650s, the overwhelming religious sentiment of the citizens appears to have remained almost entirely conservative.   A *Directory of Worship* was purchased for Newark at the time of the surrender, but its Prayer Books were hidden away rather than destroyed as the Ordinance stipulated.   There remains little evidence to suggest that the enforced alterations to Newark's liturgy and church were greeted with any enthusiasm in the town.

Newark was therefore, in many ways, a microcosm of the wider national scene and for this reason makes an excellent case study for the historian of this period.   It is intended that this work will be of interest not only to the local historian but also to historians of the period and the general reader in gaining further insight to the momentous events over the years 1640-1660.

Throughout the book where sources are quoted directly, original spellings are retained within quotations although punctuation is sometimes added to giver greater clarity. As with current usage, the New Year is taken as beginning on 1 January rather than the seventeenth century practice of assigning it to Lady Day (25 March).

A true and exact Relation of the manner of his Maiesties setting up of His Standard at Nottingham, on Munday the 22. of August 1642.

First, The forme of the Standard, as it is here figured, and who were present at the advancing of it

Secondly, The danger of setting up of former Standards, and the damage which ensued thereon.

Thirdly, A relation of all the Standards that ever were set up by any King.

Fourthly, the names of those Knights who are appointed to be the Kings Standard-bearers. With the forces that are appoynted to guard it.

Fifthly, The manner of the Kings comming first to Coventry.

Sixtly, The Cavalieres resolution and dangerous threats which they have uttered, if the King concludes a peace without them, or hearkens unto his great Councell the Parliament : Moreover how they have shared and divided London amongst themselves already.

Nottingham.

London, printed for F. Coles. 1642,

CHAPTER 1

'A very neate.... built town'[7]:
Newark in the early seventeenth century

On the 21 April 1603 King James arrived at Newark on his journey from Scotland to take possession of the English throne. His coming to Newark was greeted with widespread celebration and he was welcomed with great ceremony by the town Corporation who presented him with a large silver cup. Mr John Twentyman, a gentleman of Newark, delivered a Latin oration in praise of the king's visit to the town. This speech was greatly appreciated by the king who appointed Twentyman to the office of 'purveyor of wax for the royal household' in reward for his oration and also in recognition of his many local trade contacts.[8] Thus began the close links between the town and the Stuart dynasty, which were to be a prominent feature of Newark's life for the next seven decades. James appears to have viewed the town with great affection for in 1605 he granted the burgesses of the borough a revised charter conferring on it additional privileges including the power to draft local ordinances.[9] During his reign the king visited Newark on a further four occasions, in 1612, 1614, 1616 and 1617. The Twentyman family was again to feature prominently in the events of the Stuart dynasty during the turbulent years of the Civil War, this time in service of James's son Charles I.[10]

At the start of the seventeenth century Newark-on-Trent was the second largest town in the county of Nottingham. It was an ancient and thriving market town that still possessed its medieval walls and gates. The town lies 124 miles north of London and 21 miles north-east of Nottingham. Newark was situated at the meeting of two great highways, the Roman Fosse Way from Bath to Lincoln and the Great North Road, which linked London with the northern counties and Scotland. Known as the 'Key to the North' it commanded the crossing nearest to the Humber estuary on the river Trent, Britain's third longest river. At this time the bridge at Newark was constructed of timber and underwent major repairs in 1627 and again in 1653.[11] Considerable trade travelled along both the river and roads and the large Market Square was a centre of commerce for the surrounding parishes, bringing considerable prosperity to the town. Newark thrived on trade in the products of farming such as wool, hides, leather and the manufacture of cloth whilst the traffic of coal and corn along the river further bolstered the town's position as a regional economic centre. The river Trent divided in two a little above Newark with the smaller of the two branches running alongside the town. The river Devon joins this branch of the Trent at Newark and so the town found itself bounded by rivers on both its west and southern sides. The streets, taverns and inns were generally filled with travellers and traders who were journeying either south to London or north to York and Scotland.[12]

The name Newark is probably derived from the expression 'new works'. The 'old works' may have referred to the Roman fort of Margidnum which lay ten miles away, or, more likely, to a previous Saxon fort that is thought to have stood near the town.[13] To distinguish it from the Newark that existed near Peterborough the town's situation 'on Trent' was added to its name. As with many other settlements alongside the river Trent, Newark was built on a deposit of river gravel that raised it above the flood plain. The river cannot move this gravel (which probably originated as glacial deposits) with the result that fertile sands and clays are deposited as it winds it way around it. As a consequence wide flat meadows extend mile after mile along the river here, being some of the most fertile in the county, ideal for growing corn and for pasture.[14] At Newark the meadow and pasture lands of the town lay to the west, adjacent to the river, whilst the arable fields lay to the north, east and south of the parish. From court rolls we know that the open fields to the north of the town were called Sand, Clay and Stonepit fields – again recalling the river deposits of which they were made.[15] In 1700 there appears to have been few enclosure encroachments upon these open fields with farming being carefully monitored and controlled by the manorial court.

Newark acted as a service centre not only for traders passing through the town but also for its surrounding parishes. Amongst the Corporation miscellaneous papers for 1609 there exists a list of 'Brewers and Tipplers' which identifies 54 brewers and 24 keepers of tippling houses within Newark for that year.[16] Alongside these there were the numerous taverns and inns that provided accommodation for travellers. Brewing was therefore an essential part of the town's service industry and it would have drawn malt and barley in from the surrounding parishes. Newark was well situated for access to running water and a growing number of mills for grinding corn and fulling cloth were built along the rivers Devon and Trent. A lease dated 1534 recorded that Anthony Foster was running five corn and two fulling mills and by 1700 the number of mills would have risen considerably.[17] These mills probably serviced not only the town but also neighbouring parishes that were removed from the rivers. The Newark mills were a part of the estate of the lord of the manor and the inhabitants of the town were compelled to grind their corn at the lord's mill.[18]

In 1697 Celia Fiennes visited Newark and wrote a description of the town in her journal.

> Newark is a very neate stone built town the market place is
> very large and look'd fine, just by it is the Great Church which
> is large and with a very high spire, there is prayers twice a day
> in it; there remaines the holes in the church walls that the bullets
> made which were shott into the town in the siege laid to it by the
> Parliament army in the Civil Warrs; the castle was then
> demolished so that only the ruinated walls remaine which is
> washed by a very pretty river.[19]

The town viewed by Fiennes at the end of the seventeenth century had been greatly shaped by the events of the previous 100 years, in particular the period 1640-1660, which is the focus of this book. The extensive damage caused by the civil war was still visible, but after 1660 large parts of the town had been rebuilt in stone. The basic layout of the earlier settlement, however, was retained.

In 1600 Newark was predominantly a town of homogenous, low-roofed timber frame houses, some with large gardens. Like many medieval towns it was laid out with a well-planned regularity. At the centre of the walled town lay its vast market place, which was the focus of Newark's trade life. In 1630, 'cogles and stones' had been purchased to complete the paving of the market place thus making it the main thoroughfare for the town.[20] The medieval walls remained largely complete, but in places they were in a ruinous condition. The gates in the walls provided the main access into the town but their narrow entrances and the confined streets beyond were a cause of considerable congestion, especially on market days. The town had long spread beyond the confines of its medieval walls in ribbon developments along both North Gate and Mill Gate. The latter, running parallel with the river, was an important part of the town owing to the mills that were located beside it.

Within the old walls there were few stone buildings, the most prominent being the castle and the parish church. Thomas Magnus, a wealthy churchman, founded the Newark Grammar School in 1529 and his stone schoolhouse still stands in Appleton Gate. Beyond the walls stood the recently built stone house of the Earl of Exeter, which was situated on the site of the Spittal - an old medieval hospital which had been demolished to allow the building of the house.

As in many medieval towns, the preponderance of timber buildings, narrowing the streets with their projecting jetties, made the spread of fire a constant risk. Orders were given in 1592 and 1615 for the provision of fire-fighting equipment and throughout the seventeenth century the churchwarden's accounts periodically record the purchase or repair of buckets, ladders and drag hooks.[21]

Standing at the west-end of the town, alongside the river Trent, stood Newark Castle. Its presence and history were to have a considerable impact upon the community until its slighting in 1647. It was Alexander, Bishop of Lincoln, who had built the first stone castle over the years 1123 to 1148. This was a fortified Episcopal palace built around a rectangular courtyard or inner ward. The gatehouse, which still stands today, was the first part of the castle to be built and is a fine example of medieval construction. The substantial curtain wall, which still stands to the height of 75 feet on the river side, had towers at each of its four corners although only the south-east tower survives today. The castle was to remain in the hands of the Bishops of Lincoln for over 400 years until ownership was transferred to the Crown after the Reformation. During the fifteenth and sixteenth century improvements were made to render the castle less of a military stronghold and more akin to a nobleman's fine residence. In 1603, James I stayed at the castle on his journey to London from Scotland. His son Charles I also stayed there on several occasions during the 1630s and 1640s, suggesting that Newark castle remained in good repair throughout the first four decades of the seventeenth century. The imposing presence of the castle served both as a reminder of the Crown's presence and the strategic importance of Newark for travel, communication and trade.[22]

The spire of St. Mary Magdalene parish church can be seen for miles in all directions and attached to it is an excellent example of a medieval church. To the seventeenth century inhabitants of Newark their church was a source of considerable civic pride.

With an internal length of 222 ft, this large church was well equipped to serve the town as its sole place of worship at the start of the seventeenth century. The tower and spire date to the thirteenth and fourteenth century but the rest of the church, with its tall columns and very large windows, characteristic of the perpendicular style, was built in the fifteenth century.[23] At the Reformation its medieval guild chapels and furnishings were swept away and its richly decorated walls whitewashed over. A sense of space and grandeur conveyed via its slim perpendicular pillars supporting a richly carved roof continued to impress both worshipper and visitor throughout the seventeenth century. In 1677 the local magistrate and historian Dr Robert Thoroton wrote 'it is now one of the finest churches I ever saw'.[24] The ornate sixteenth century rood screen, separating the chancel from the nave, survived the upheavals of Protestant reform (albeit not without damage) and acted as a focal point through which to view the altar. Medieval brasses and monuments continued to adorn the walls and floor of the church and we know from churchwarden's records that there was an organ in the church until 1646. A choir of six choristers and their master, meanwhile, enriched the liturgy and trained at the nearby Song School, which had been established by Thomas Magnus in 1532.[25] An entry in the churchwarden's accounts for 1630 suggests that the choristers were robed in dark blue gowns faced with white cotton.[26] (Blue was also the livery colour for Newark Borough Corporation officers). Most of the church's stained glass was destroyed at the Reformation but some still remained to be seen *in situ* during the first part of the seventeenth century. For the first five decades of the seventeenth century the parish of Newark was served by just six vicars, suggesting a considerable degree of continuity within the parish over this period.

Up until 1547 Newark was part of the manor owned by the Bishops of Lincoln. In that year, however, an exchange of land took place which transferred ownership to the Crown in the reign of Edward VI. In 1549 the first Charter of Newark was enacted at Westminster with corporate authority within the town being vested in an alderman and twelve assistants. Prior to this date the Guilds of Corpus Christi and St. Trinity appear to have held considerable authority over the day to day running of the church (and hence town affairs). In fact six of the new aldermen were chosen from the Trinity Guild.[27] The fifth charter of 1626 changed the alderman and his twelve assistants into a mayor and twelve aldermen and also allowed for the appointment of a town recorder. In all other respects, however, the basis of local control remained unaltered from the first charter of 1549. By the seventeenth century most of the town's economic activity and public affairs were clearly under the command of the Corporation. The responsibilities of the aldermen were outlined in an order of 1613 which stated that they were

> Appoynted to sit together in the Court of Record and to walke ye
> Towne every market & fayre daye at night in their severall
> Disneys [wards][28]

Election to the body of aldermen was solely in the hands of the thirteen members of the Corporation and by the seventeenth century it had become, in effect, a self-perpetuating oligarchy. An individual who was elected to office but refused to serve could be punished by the Corporation. This usually involved a short period of imprisonment and a heavy fine. In 1606, the sum was £20, but if you accepted an office and then refused or failed to attend to your duties the fine rose to £40.[29] The task was certainly onerous and one can sympathise with the number of instances recorded in the Borough minutes of individuals refusing to accept the position. Service as an alderman was considered to be for life although release was allowed for those 'in respecte of sickness and other weakness in bodie' as well as for those who had moved away from the town.[30]

The mayor and aldermen played a leading role in the control of trade in the town and also in the appointment of Freemen. A bond of £5 had to be paid to the Corporation by anyone who moved into the town and sought to practice any trade. The Corporation also monitored apprenticeships. On the completion of their training, apprentices were obliged to appear before the mayor and aldermen to swear an oath of allegiance to the king, affirm their willingness to abide by the rules of the Borough and pay the tolls. Only after completion of the ceremony could they be recorded as Freemen.

The Corporation of Newark did not have sole authority within the town; it shared some control with the Lord of the Manor. The owner of the manor had all the profits of certain annual fairs and also the right of 'sucken', which obliged local inhabitants to take their grain to his mills for grinding. Many townspeople, and even the Corporation, leased land and properties from the manor. Ownership of the manor belonged to the king (and later Queen Henrietta Maria) until 1649. Following the execution of Charles I in that year, control passed to the Parliamentarian administrators. Despite the upheavals of the mid-seventeenth century the transfer of manorial lands between freeholders and copyholders appears to have continued in the traditional way. Whilst the manor proved to be a considerable source of income for the Crown, it does not seem to have greatly interfered with the Corporation's administration of town affairs, providing it received its dues and payments.

The post of mayor was filled from the ranks of aldermen. On Easter Monday the name of two candidates was presented to the whole body and an election was held. Service as mayor was for a period of twelve months and no one was expected to serve more than once in every seven years. Although the post enjoyed considerable social prestige it also incurred substantial personal cost, both in time and money. When subsidies had to be paid, the mayor was usually the first and highest contributor and he was expected to attend and chair all the meetings of the Corporation. The mayor, however, did receive a small financial allowance. At the start of the seventeenth century he was paid out of the town funds the sum of £6.13s.4d as well as 'the comodite and profitt of both Fayres and of the lease of the borough courtes and other fynes issues, amerciaments as before time hath bene accustomed'.[31] From 1614 a cloak of 'blacke broade cloath' was provided for the mayor with a replacement being purchased in 1633 at a cost of £1.11s.6d. The aldermen also had their 'Tippetts of velvet' which they were obliged to wear on civic occasions.

A local ordinance of 1550 introduced a second body of men into the government of the town. This group also numbered twelve and was known as the Second Company. Its individual members were known as coadjutors. Their principal duty was to act as assistants to the mayor and aldermen and from within their ranks future aldermen were selected. The appointment of men to this second body resided entirely in the hands of the mayor and aldermen and refusal to serve in the office again attracted the usual heavy fine.

According to the Charter of 1626 it was necessary for the Corporation to appoint a Recorder, 'one good and discreet man learned in the laws of England'.[32] His task was to provide the officials with legal advice and counsel when it was either required or sought. Throughout most of the Civil War the town recorder was Gilbert Boone, who was a sergeant-at-law and an avowed Royalist. On the surrender of the town in 1646 he was quickly dismissed and by 1651 the post was being occupied by Colonel John Hutchinson, the former Parliamentarian Governor of Nottingham.

Alongside the Corporation and Second Company there were a number of minor civic offices that assisted in the administration of the town. The office of beadle, also known as the Alderman's Assistant was there to act as a servant to the Corporation and also summon all persons whom the aldermen wished to appear before them. He was paid an annual salary and also received a portion of the fines imposed either upon Corporation members or commoners. The duty of collecting these fines was allocated to the two sergeants at mace.[33] Two chamberlains were appointed each for a period of two years but never simultaneously, to administer the town's finances. The mayor was responsible for appointing two town constables whose prime duty was to police the town and the maintaining of the public peace. All of these officials were supervised by and accountable to the mayor and aldermen, and together they ensured the day-to-day running of the town and its affairs in the seventeenth century.

From the twelfth century onwards, the inhabitants of Newark had been well served by a number of charitable endowments. The majority were established in the seventeenth century and either provided for the fabric and services of the church or for the relief of the poor. In table 1.1 the date and purpose of these main charities are given. Many of these bequests consisted of properties and land in and around the town of Newark, which were to be administered on behalf of the town by the mayor and aldermen. The proceeds of the rents and leases were to be used by them to meet the benefactor's intentions. Alongside the parish provision of 'poor relief', these charities probably played an important part in the life of Newark's 'poorer sort'. In financial terms they possibly kept a number of widows and orphans above the level of destitution, although it is also clear from their purposes that improvement of the town's poor was viewed as much in terms of education as material relief. The preaching of sermons 'could equip the poor' to better their lot.

Table 1.1 Charitable endowments in use during the seventeenth century

Date	Benefactor	Purpose
1532	Thomas Magnus	Grammar School and Song School
1532	Robert Brown	Repairs at church and good works in town
1556	William Phyllypott	Provide alms house and maintenance for 5 poor men
1612	William Bethell	6s.8d for sermon & 13s.4d for poor each year
1619	Mr Chapman	Houses for four poor widows and maintenance
1623	John Lilley	£126 per annum for poor children in Jersey School
1644	Hercules Clay	Annual sermon and distribution of bread to poor
1655	John Johnson	Repairs of church and £5 per annum for poor
1657	William Watson	Annual sermon on Christmas day
1663	John Martin	Coals for the poor at Christmas
1675	Emma Watson	Corn for the poor
1675	Richard Lamb	25s per annum for the poor
1678	Anthony Collingwood	Maintenance of divine worship at church
1679	Earl of Scarsdale	Preaching of two annual sermons
1690	Lady Francis Leeke	£100 for poor and £200 for church plate

During the chaotic time of the Civil Wars most of these charitable endowments appear to have continued to function, albeit on a reduced income because of the difficulties of collecting rents during times of siege. Once the war had ended, these endowments gradually returned to their pre-war incomes.

The size of Newark's population in the seventeenth century has proved difficult to assess with any degree of certainty. Professor A. C. Wood suggests that the seventy burials recorded over the period 1599-1600 indicate a population of over 2000 at the start of the century.[34] Other work on parish register data has yielded an estimated population of around 2,774 but the multiplier used is now generally regarded as too high. Research based on the 1674 hearth tax returns has estimated a population of about 1,444, but this low figure possibly reflects an under-recording of households by up to 25 per cent.[35] It seems safe to assume that the town over which the Corporation presided had a population between 2,000-2,400 over the first four decades of the seventeenth century. The events and consequences of the Civil War appear to have reduced the population to lower than 1640 figures during the second part of the century. This may well have been a consequence of both disease and famine and may account for the lower population estimates obtained from the hearth tax returns. This development is explored later in the book.[36]

The political consequences of Charles I's personal rule and the calling of two Parliaments between 1640 and 1641 also had an impact on the everyday life of Newark citizens. The most controversial and significant of Charles' impositions during the 1630s was the extension of the ship money levy. From being originally an occasional tax imposed on ports and coastal counties to finance the navy, ship money was extended to all English counties in 1635, and by 1637 it had become a semi-permanent source of revenue for the Crown. The first writ was issued in 1635 and Newark was assessed at £110, a figure that initially the town appeared to meet.[37] The following year the levy was increased to £120 and this too appears to have been raised, although probably with less grace. By 1637 the economic circumstances of the town had deteriorated considerably and the further sum of £120 proved difficult to raise. By 18 September the town had managed to pay only £50 of the total.[38] By the end of the first quarter of 1638 the outstanding amount had been reduced to £20 but the Corporation claimed that £13.6s.8d of this was owed by the Earl of Berkshire, the Earl of Exeter and Squire Leeke.[39] All three of these substantial landowners contested the claim that they held rateable property within the town and hence were liable to pay. The Earl of Exeter wrote to the Privy Council 'my answer is that my house is not of that town, nor have I any land within their liberties for which they ought to assess me'.[40] The failure of these leading gentry to meet the town's demands placed an unrealistic financial burden on the rest of Newark's citizens.

By 1638, growing national economic hardship and lower naval requirements led the Crown to impose a much smaller national levy. The sum imposed on Newark amounted to £45, but even this lower sum proved to be too much for the Borough Corporation and they took the significant action of petitioning the Star Chamber. In their address

> They complained of being over-rated towards the business of shipping,
> viz. smallness of trade; the poorness of people; the absence of gentlemen
> and able men that dwelt there and contributed to former taxes but are

now removed; that £45 considering the weak estate of the town is more
than double the proportion laid on other towns in that country.[41]

The Sheriff of Nottingham was instructed by the Privy Council to examine the circumstances of Newark and ascertain its ability to pay the levies as set. Whilst this review was underway it did not halt the imposition of a further £120 for the next financial year. The deteriorating political situation and the outbreak of the Bishop's Wars in 1639, coupled with the recall of Parliament in 1640, meant that across the nation very little of the 1639 levy was raised and this would certainly have been the case in Newark. Ironically in 1640 the Sheriff responded to the Privy Council

I took into consideration the poor estate of Newark and in accordance
with your former directions…have eased the town of £40 and imposed
it upon the body of the county.[42]

The ship money levies imposed on Newark created considerable hardship for the town's citizens, especially in the absence of wealthy gentry to lighten the load. The Sheriff of Nottingham grudgingly acknowledged this fact as a problem countywide. In a further letter to the Privy Council in 1637 he remarked,

There have been many distresses taken, and much trouble in collecting
the money. There is indeed no trading in the county (and) the country
people most commonly live by husbandry and hard work.[43]

Whilst ship money has been identified by a number of historians as a factor in creating an opposition to Charles' Personal Rule, in Newark it appears to have had little long-term effect on the town's subsequent allegiance once Civil War erupted. It certainly created hardship and dissatisfaction during the 1630s but in no way coloured the town's commitment to the king once his standard was raised in 1642.

It was Scotland that proved to be the catalyst for the slide into Civil War across the British Isles. Here dissatisfaction with Charles' religious policy, especially the imposition of the Prayer Book on the national Presbyterian Church, led to open revolt in 1639. The Anglo-Scottish wars of 1639 and 1640, popularly known as the Bishop's Wars, had a tremendous impact upon English politics and the everyday life of Newark's citizens. During the first part of 1639 orders were issued to the lords lieutenants in each county to prepare the trained bands for mobilisation. These bands comprised part-time amateur soldiers drawn from every village and town, organised on a county basis. Each county was also required to provide a quota of men for the national army, which in April 1639 was assembling at York. For the people of Newark the first impact of this development was in the form of a further taxation levy known as coat and conduct money. This tax covered the costs of food, arms, ammunition and uniforms for the conscripts as they were escorted to the rendezvous at York. As Newark lay on the Great North Road it would have experienced a steady stream of soldiers passing through on their way north. Little evidence remains of the financial implications that this brought to the town but glimpses are given in the remaining fragmentary Borough records. In March 1639 the town paid £7.4s in wages, £1.17s.4d for powder and match and 12s for four pairs of shoes for its eight 'pressed soldiers'. In 1640 the sum of 15s.6d had to be spent on 'levied soldiers' with a further £1.12s on repairing the town's armour.[44] Though these additional outlays would have come as a further blow to the town's economy they were merely a foretaste of the expenses that lay ahead over the years of the Civil War.

The 1630s proved to be a time of financial hardship for Newark, as for a number of towns across the country. There appears to have been a downturn in trade along the river Trent causing hardship for many of the town's merchants and this coincided with the departure of a number of gentry families. Further pressures were caused by a succession of average harvests over the decade. 1630 was certainly a bad year with dearth being recorded in many parts of the country; 1632 and 1637 were described as 'deficient harvests'. It was not until 1639 that a harvest was once again considered to be good.[45] Such generally poor harvests would have contributed to the decline of the grain trade along the Trent. Coupled with growing rates of taxation, through ship money and coat and conduct levies, Newark approached the 1640s having experienced a number of financially lean years. The economic, social and administrative state of the town in 1642 gave no hint to its coming importance to the Royalist cause over the next six years. Whilst there may have been some factors that contributed to its loyalty to the king, this chapter has clearly shown that there were no obvious financial or social features to make this commitment a foregone conclusion.

CHAPTER 2

'The warre between the king and parliament':
Newark, 1642-1646

On the 2 March 1642, despite the protestations of his Parliament, Charles I left the vicinity of London, moving northwards to establish his court at York. He was not to see the capital again until his trial and execution in 1649. By the spring of 1642 the relationship between the king and Parliament had all but broken down, with major differences in opinion over control of the military and the use of the royal prerogative. With the king being absent, parliament attempted to take control of the trained bands eventually issuing a Military Bill without the approval of the king. Charles responded promptly to this slight of his royal authority by issuing Commissions of Array to the lords lieutenants of counties and known supporters instructing them to call out the militia for the service of the king. The descent into war now gathered pace. On the 12 July Charles visited Newark and addressed the gentry and freeholders of Nottinghamshire seeking to gain their support for his cause. In a conciliatory speech he told them

> I ask nothing of you (although your demeanour gives me good evidence that
> you are not willing to deny) but to preserve your own affections for the
> religion and the laws established. I will justify and protect these affections
> and will live and die with you in that quarrel.[46]

The king moved on to Lincoln that day but Lord Newark, the king's lords lieutenant in Nottinghamshire, remained behind to address the trained bands who mustered at Newark the following day. The king returned to Newark on 17 August when he was moving towards Nottingham to raise his royal standard. This was the time-honoured symbol for the king's supporters to assemble for military service and as such was a declaration of war against Parliament. Thus the first Civil War (1642-1646) formally began in Nottinghamshire and was also to end in the county on the 5 May 1646 when the king surrendered himself to the Scottish army then besieging Newark. Thus it was that the market town of Newark found itself at the very centre of a conflict which would impact substantially on both its present and future.

Newark was to be of strategic importance for the Royalist cause as a communications centre. Retaining control of the town meant that a road route could be maintained between the king's HQ at Oxford and the important northern towns of York and Newcastle. Possessing a strong castle and controlling the passage of the Trent for a considerable distance it remained a Royalist fortress throughout the first Civil War, successfully repulsing three major sieges by the Parliamentarian armies. All of these factors have meant that Newark has occupied the interest of historians over a number of centuries and a variety of comprehensive military accounts of these times have been produced.[47] These provide an excellent overview of events in a chronological and detailed manner, but the availability of new sources – particularly in the form of Corporation papers and the previously unused eyewitness account of John Twentyman and military account book of the regiment of Colonel William Staunton - provide us with much additional information. Using this collection of older histories and the new primary sources mentioned above, this chapter will construct a fresh narrative of events involving the town in the years 1642-1646.

On the 22 August 1642, Charles I raised his Standard at Nottingham Castle. The initial response to this rallying call, both within Nottinghamshire and nationally, proved to be very disappointing for the king with recruits for his army coming in very slowly and in small numbers. Of the troops that were recruited in Nottinghamshire, 'an extraordinary number for a single town [came] from Newark'.[48] These included a Regiment of Foot raised by Gervase Holles (MP for Grimsby), who was then living in the town[49] and a Regiment of Horse raised by John Bellasis from his estates in Yorkshire and at Holme near Newark.[50] Likewise William Staunton provided a Regiment of Horse from his tenants and neighbours in and around Staunton, which lay about 7 miles south of Newark.[51] From these few examples it is easy to see why Newark achieved such a high profile during these early days of recruiting, and the strength of Royalist fervour which pervaded the town. Within the city of Nottingham by contrast, support for the king was minimal and there remained a quiet, unexpressed sympathy for the Parliament among many of the town's inhabitants.

Two rejected peace missions initiated by the king and Parliament's subsequent declaration that individuals who supported the Royalist cause would incur financial penalties, added fresh impetus to the king's recruitment campaign as the nation became further divided by the extreme nature of pronouncements. Even so, the presence of a Parliamentarian army of 20,000 at Northampton forced the king to leave Nottingham for Shrewsbury on the 13 September. Here he hoped to gain additional levies from the west and Wales where Royalist support was strong. As the Nottinghamshire Royalists and their regiments of local men marched away with the king's army, they left a power vacuum in the county of their origin. They did not return until late November 1642 following the Edgehill campaign, and Parliamentarians in the east Midlands used this time to secure their own power base in the region. At the end of October Sir John Gell secured the town of Derby for Parliament, whilst in the county of Lincolnshire Parliamentarian sympathies became well rooted. In Nottinghamshire, meanwhile, two local gentry, John Hutchinson and Francis Pierrepont were active in co-ordinating the cause for Parliament.

Over the months of September to November 1642 the citizens of Newark cannot have failed to view the growing influence of Parliamentarian supporters in Nottinghamshire with anything but concern. With a number of their local gentry and men folk away in the service of the king, and no soldiers remaining in the town, it was left to ordinary citizens to defend themselves should any attempt be made by Parliamentarians to take the town. Little evidence survives to document what was actually happening in Newark during these early months of the war, but the account left by Newark citizen John Twentyman does record a hitherto unidentified skirmish for the town involving two troops of Parliamentarian horse from Lincoln:

> Our familie was loyall & true to his late Majestie Charles the
> First and gave the decision to make that Town of Newarke a
> Garrison, Thus Two troopes of Horse came from Lincoln under
> command of them who were for the Parliment, and faced the Towne
> upon Beacon Hill, it was reported in the town that they would come
> and plunder the towne. One of my uncles having been Ensign to
> Captain Rossell and an old drum being in the House, but the head
> broken, my Grandmother charged my uncle Edward Twentyman
> upon her blessing to take it out and commanded Edward Foster her
> grandchild to beat an alarm, and see who would stand for king Charles

> & their own Defence. They came together unanimously with forks and
> spitts and what weapons they had, for very few guns were among them
> and resolved to defend themselves as well as they could and upon what
> notice or feare I know not, those troopes withdrew and made no attempt.[52]

It was entirely as a result of this bravery shown by the townsfolk that Newark remained available for local Royalists to establish a garrison in the town on their return following the Edgehill campaign.

It was not until November 1642, however, that the king, still ensconced in Shrewsbury sent Sir John Digby (the Sheriff of Nottingham) and other leading Royalists back to the county with instructions to secure the shire. To this end Digby and his cohorts established their headquarters at the town of Newark and summoned a meeting of the county's JPs on 10 December 1642.[53] John Hutchinson was one of the magistrates summoned to the meeting, but on being warned that it was a trap to arrest leading Parliamentarians he refused to attend.[54] Warning the town of Nottingham of a possible occupation by Digby and the Royalists, Hutchinson was able to enlist 700 men into a defensive regiment, which was placed under the command of his brother George. Then, with additional assistance from Sir John Gell, he secured Nottingham for Parliament and established a garrison at the castle. This development left Newark once again exposed to attack causing Digby to send to the Earl of Newcastle requesting the establishment of a Royalist garrison in the town. Between 18 and 23 December 1642 around 4,000 Horse under the command of Sir John Henderson, 'a Scotchman', arrived in Newark from the Earl's army in the north. Henderson, as head of the garrison, was appointed first military governor of the town. Thus it was that by Christmas 1642, two opposing garrisons – at Newark and Nottingham - had been established in the county, each poised for action.

One of the first tasks confronting the new Governor of Newark was to strengthen the town defences. The town already possessed a medieval town wall, but this was dilapidated and breached in many places. The town, moreover, had spread way beyond the circuit of these walls and a new series of defensive structures was clearly required. In a matter of ten weeks, Henderson oversaw the construction by soldiers and able-bodied townspeople, of an entirely new earthen rampart and ditch, surrounding the most strategic parts of the town.

The feat of constructing the ramparts in such a short space of time was undeniably remarkable, but to one observer at least, they were not likely to prove infallible in defending the town from attack. It was John Twentyman who noted in his narrative that:

> ...they made a garrison of it, takeing in only the round of the
> Town and leaving out Milngate and the best streete for building
> (and) Northgate with the Earle of Exeter's House. And most pitifull
> works they were, very low and thin and a drie ditch which most men
> might easily leap upon the East and South.

Within a matter of months Twentyman's prediction was to be put to the test.

Parliamentarian victories at Leeds and Wakefield in February 1643 forced the Earl of Newcastle to withdraw most of his forces from Newark in order to address this reversal in the north. Henderson was left with only local levies and volunteers to defend the town, though these may have numbered around a 1,000 strong. The time was right for local Parliamentarians to attempt to wrest control of the town from Royalist hands. On 27 February 1643, Major-General Thomas Ballard approached Newark with, according to Royalist accounts, 6,000 men and ten pieces of ordinance. This was an army of trained soldiers who were severely to test the resolve of Newark's citizens and the strength of the new defences. Twentyman was most certainly in the town at the time of this attack and wrote many years later his recollection of the event.

> The Parliament forces came against it under the command of
> Major Generall Ballard, who had served in forreign warrs and such
> were so renowned that they were thought able to do wonders among
> us in the beginning of our unhappy Discords. Sir John Henderson a
> Scotchman who had also been abroad in forreign service was then
> Governor of the Town. The Parliament's forces came to the Spittle or
> towards it, which occasioned both it and Norgate to be sett on fire.
> Then they made some attempt to enter at Balderton Gate, but were
> beat off and the Towns-men won 2 or 3 little peices from them which
> greatly encouraged them. They attempted some other parts of the
> Town, but not in diverse places at once, for they within had so few guns
> that they were forced who had them to run with them to the place of
> assault as Colonell Henderson ordered and directed, who rode upon a
> white horse and encouraged the soldiers and kept in continuall motion

upon his horse that the enemie might not take mark at him. Low and
bad (as I have said) works. God at this time preserved the Town, for
the Parliament forces drew off and went away and they imputed the not
winning of the Town at this time to the trechery of Major General
Ballard.

Twentyman's account supplies us with many helpful insights but fails to mention
how the Royalists' defence strategy was shaped by the poor quality of their
munitions. Initially Henderson took up a position on Beacon Hill with his cavalry
hoping to stop the attackers before they reached the town's new defences. His lack
of artillery, however, forced him to retreat behind the defences and so the fighting
was brought right into the vicinity of Newark itself.

For the people of Newark this would have been their first real experience of warfare.
As Twentyman's account shows they were ill prepared for the destructive nature of
the fighting and ill equipped to retaliate. Their experience would have been similar
to most communities across England, where there had been no local experience of
conflict since the Tudor Rebellions or the Wars of the Roses. Whilst military
manuals had been popular over the first four decades of the seventeenth century, the
actual experience of warfare was limited to a small number of gentry who had
fought overseas in European conflicts. As a result such individuals were held in
high esteem at the start of the Civil War and their experience, and the confidence it
engendered, were much sought after by both sides. This fact is clearly noted in the
Twentyman account of this initial action at Newark. Henderson's cool and
authoritative manner in the midst of chaotic events was essential in inspiring the
garrison in its purpose. Twentyman noted with glee that Ballard's so-called
experience contributed little to the Parliamentarian venture and that, subsequently,
he was made the scapegoat for its failure. Lucy Hutchinson also suggested in her
account that Ballard's indecision also contributed to the Parliamentarian's failure
to take the town.

A second feature, to which Twentyman's account draws attention, is the scarcity of
weapons available across the country at the start of hostilities. This was particularly
true of the Royalist forces to which the arms and munitions of the Ordinance Office
at the Tower of London and the well-stocked magazines at Hull and Portsmouth

were unavailable being already in the hands of Parliament.[55] Throughout the whole of the Midlands the equipping of locally raised forces, by both sides, proved difficult during these early stages. Later in the war at Newark, workshops for the production of munitions and weapons were established at Mill Gate. We know about this from the later proceedings of the Committee for Advance of Money Causes where in 1650 Lady Saville was examined. She was accused of procuring in 1644 '20 cases of pistols made at Newark to raise the siege at Pontefract'.[56] At the start of the war no such resources were available and many had to fight armed only with clubs or pitchforks as Twentyman's account shows. Thus the winning of '2 or 3 little pieces [of ordinance]' by the townsmen of Newark takes on great significance. Indeed the shortage of muskets in the town forced the soldiers to move around the defences to intercept the next expected attack.

Although the Newark Royalists had inflicted a humiliating defeat upon the Parliamentarians, there were real causes for concern. Whereas the earthen ramparts had not been breached the attackers had been able to approach them with relative ease. It was clear that over the next twelve months much more substantial defences were needed if the town was to be defended against further attacks. This would include extending the defences to bring previously unsecured parts of Mill Gate into the circuit of defensive works. Around Newark meanwhile, the five petty or outpost garrisons established at Belvoir Castle, Norwell House, Shelford Manor, Thurgaton Priory and Wiverton Hall were all strengthened and provisioned so as to provide an outer defence network for the town. This extensive building project continued throughout the year and well into 1644. Twentyman provides details of the defence works constructed in the immediate vicinity of the town.

> After this they began to make new works very high and strong and set up
> a great skonse in my Dove Coate Close (called the king's sconse) a
> footstep whereof is seen by the ditch left in it and at this time they
> secured the street called Milngate. These works were begun when
> his Majesties Forces were Masters of the Field, and according to humane
> judgment (but the Lord ruleth over all, and further appeared in his anger
> against us for our sins) they might have marched to London, into the
> associate Counties and have placed the king in his throne.

From March 1643 through to the end of the year, Newark's fortunes were intrinsically linked to the successes and setbacks experienced by the northern Royalist army under the command of the Earl of Newcastle. At the beginning of March, Newcastle began a successful campaign to reverse the fortunes of Parliament in the north whilst at the same time he sent his cousin, Charles Cavendish, to strengthen the Royalist garrison at Newark.[57] On the 23 March, Cavendish and Newark forces under the command of the Governor John Henderson stormed the town of Grantham and defeated a Parliamentarian force of 1,500 men. Many prisoners were taken but more importantly the arsenal at Newark was replenished with many captured weapons. By the end of the month Lincolnshire Royalists had regained control of Stamford and the Newark horse had control of that county, right up to the walls of Lincoln.

In London, Parliamentarian leaders viewed the rise of Royalist fortunes in the east Midlands with increasing concern. On the 26 April, John Hutchinson went in person to acquaint Parliament with the precarious state of the Nottingham garrison, which he described as being in a 'weak and languishing condition'.[58] As a consequence, troops from Derby and Huntingdon, the latter under the command of Oliver Cromwell, were dispatched to Nottingham to strengthen the garrison. Overall command of all these soldiers was given to Lord Grey of Groby. A Royalist force from Newark under the command of Cavendish attempted to thwart Cromwell's march to Nottingham but at a skirmish at Grantham on the 13 May a headlong charge by the latter's horse scattered their Royalist opponents and they safely reached their destination.

Although Parliament had secured the county town, the Royalists at Newark had control of most of Nottinghamshire and large parts of Lincolnshire. This meant that they could collect assessments and taxes to fund their war effort from villages right up to the very gates of Nottingham itself. The Royalists at Newark held a great muster on the 29 May of at least 38 troops of horse and dragoons, which amounted to around 2,000 men.[59] This may have been held in order to secure a passage for Queen Henrietta Maria to travel to the town from the north. The queen eventually arrived in Newark at the head of a 4,500 strong army on the 16 June. She was to remain in the town until the 3 July and on her departure she left behind 2,000 foot and 20 companies of horse to secure the region for the king.[60] Emboldened by this new strength, the Newark garrison took part in three unsuccessful attempts on the garrison at Nottingham between June and September.

Elsewhere in the region, meanwhile, following a surprise raid on 20 July 1643 Lord Willoughby of Parnham captured the Lincolnshire town of Gainsborough for Parliament. Gainsborough held a strategic position in the Midlands, controlling the passage into Lincolnshire from Yorkshire. In turn, the loss of Gainsborough severely limited access to Newark by the Earl of Newcastle. In order to retain their new acquisition, Parliament sent troops under the command of Oliver Cromwell and Sir John Meldrum to strengthen the Gainsborough garrison. The Royalists responded promptly with a force dispatched from Newark whilst the whole of Newcastle's army moved south to support the attack. The Newark forces arrived first and after a brief battle were routed and their commander, Charles Cavendish, was killed. Just as the Parliamentarians were about to celebrate their victory, however, Newcastle arrived from the north with overwhelming numbers and retook the town. What had been a defeat for the Newark forces was turned into a stunning victory – a victory that was to mark the zenith of Royalist fortunes in the east Midlands.

The autumn of 1643, however, witnessed a revival of Parliamentarian fortunes in Lincolnshire, which the Newark garrison could do little to stem. On 11 October Cromwell routed the Royalist horse under the command of Witherington and Henderson at Winceby and not long after the towns of Lincoln and Gainsborough fell, forcing the Earl of Newcastle to abandon his siege of Hull. As a consequence of this series of disasters, Sir John Henderson was dismissed as Governor of Newark. Sir Richard Byron, a local man from Strelley in Nottinghamshire, replaced him. Twentyman provides us with a contemporary account of the battle of Winceby in his memoirs and also sheds a little light on how infighting between Royalist commanders at Newark could lead to disaster.

> …The Earl of Manchester then General of the Parliament Army for
> those parts marched with his army out of the associated Counties and
> Cromwell with him, and 3 miles from Horncastle (my native place) at
> a town called Winsby, the Lord Witherington would needes encounter

them, though Sir John Henderson was utterly against it who was
comander in chiefe, untill the other provoked him by telling him
he was a coward, and then his judgment yielded to his reputation
and honour, but the victory soon fell to the Parlimenteers.

Following his withdrawal from the siege of Hull on 12 October, the Earl of
Newcastle billeted his army close to his country seat at Welbeck, allowing Newark
to enjoy an increased level of protection during this resurgence of Parliamentarian
fortunes in Lincolnshire.

In September 1643 an alliance was formed between the English and the Scots
Parliaments through the signing of a Solemn League and Covenant. Under this
agreement the Scots undertook to supply military assistance to their neighbours,
crossing the border on 19 January 1644 to fight for its new allies. As Newcastle
gathered up his forces to march northwards to meet this new threat, Newark was
left to fight alone. Protecting the Royalist cause in Nottinghamshire, 1644 proved
to be the town's *annus horribilis*.

With Newcastle's army occupied in confronting the Scots, local Parliamentarians
could concentrate their attention on Newark. Throughout February 1644
Parliamentarian forces encroached ever nearer to the town with the Borough
minutes recording that a siege finally began on the 29 of the month.[61] The besieging
army consisted of between 5,000 and 8,000 men, drawn from the counties of
Lincolnshire, Leicestershire, Nottinghamshire and Derbyshire, under the command
of Sir John Meldrum. Of this total around 2,000 was horse. Most of the Royalist
horse at Newark had been sent away to neighbouring garrisons before the siege
began and so the defence of the town was left to 1,200 foot and six troop of horse.
The siege began with Meldrum's forces taking control of the ruined Spittal building
on North Gate, although complete encirclement of the town was not achieved until
6 March. By that date Parliamentarian forces had gained control of the Island,
which lay just to the west of the town. Here they established a fort at Muskham
Bridge on the route of the Great North Road.

The situation at Newark was dire and for three weeks it awaited a relieving force. Heavy attacks were repulsed on the 8 March and the Royalist defenders mounted at least two large sallies. The lasting memory of this time for Twentyman, as it probably was for most civilians, was of the heavy bombardment they experienced every night at midnight when '13 pieces of ordinance' and two mortars rained down death and destruction upon the town.

Newark was essential for the Royalist cause and so could not be left to its fate. It was a route for communication between Oxford and York and it protected the rear of Newcastle's army as it confronted the Scots. It was to his own nephew Prince Rupert that Charles I turned to save the garrison. By 16 March Rupert was instructing Lord Loughborough at Ashby de la Zouch to prepare victuals for the passing of his army as it came to lift the siege. Loughborough also managed to secure a further 1,500 horse and 1,200 musketeers for Rupert at Ashby and persuaded Major-General Porter to come to him with a further 1,000 horse and 600 musketeers.[62] Meldrum sent Sir Edward Hartrop with a force to intercept Porter before he reached Ashby but a mixture of incompetence and dithering led to failure at Cotes Bridge and a hasty retreat for the Parliamentarians back to Meldrum's army camped before Newark.

Rupert arrived at Newark on the morning of the 21 March with a vanguard of his horse. The rest of his army, which in total amounted to around 3,000 horse and slightly less foot, arrived later. On paper both armies were of similar size, but dissension and jealousies between rival commanders tore Meldrum's army apart. The suddenness of Rupert's appearance gave Meldrum no time to lift the siege and withdraw. He had no choice but to stay and fight. John Twentymen stood on the top of St Mary's spire and watched the unfolding battle, providing us with one of the few eyewitness accounts of the conflict.[63]

> I was in it all that seige. They shott after they had formed their League
> 13 peices of ordinance every night and 2 Bomballs about 12 and one
> of the clock. Prince Rupert came and raised this seige. (I saw the
> Engagement from the Pinacles or steeple.) They of the Parliament drew
> up their horse into one main Body and 2 wings under the brow of Beacon
> Hill against that place where Spittle stood, and where all their Infantry

were enskonsed and there they had a Bridge of Boats over the Trent. The Prince charged one wing coming with fury upon them from Codington ward, and after the charge both retired that wing to the main body and the Prince with his up the Hill, and presently he came down upon the other wing and they did as before on both sides. Upon the 3d assault the Prince coming with his whole Body upon theirs totally routed them and fell so in with them they made a length from the hill to Spittle; there the Horse would have broke into their own Foot, but they shott to keep them out. Many fled over the Bridge of Boates and all would have gone, but they were forced to stay some that they might make the better Composition for themselves and they were so, and did leave all their armes behind them and march away. Thus the Lord delivered us this time also. This was the second seige.

Twentyman claimed to have witnessed three cavalry charges, whereas other witnesses speak of only two. Whatever the number, the important thing is that on the final charge the Parliamentarian horse were routed and fled over the 'bridge of boats' on to the Island, leaving the foot at the Spittal to fight alone. On Rupert's instruction a body of horse and foot sallied on to the Island from the garrison and managed to capture Muskham Fort after its defenders fled. Meldrum's escape route was now cut off and he had no choice but to negotiate for terms. The victorious Royalists captured between 3,000-4,000 muskets, 11 canons and 2 mortars with little less than 100 casualties.[64] It was a stunning victory for Rupert, which earned the prince the grateful thanks of Charles and restored the prominence of Newark in the local conflict.

As a consequence of this victory, Lincoln, Gainsborough and Sleaford were hastily abandoned by their Parliamentarian garrisons and the town of Newark was to enjoy a degree of unimpaired operation for nearly six months. It was events elsewhere in the country that were next to impinge upon the affairs of Newark, beginning with the defeat of the king's Northern Army and Prince Rupert at Marston Moor on 2 July 1644. From then onwards the people of Newark must have sensed that to all intents and purposes they stood alone.

Initially, the collapse of the Royalist cause in the north actually made the town stronger as soldiers from surrendered garrisons made their way to Newark swelling the size of its garrison.[65] After the defeat of the Northern Royalist Army however,

Newark's days were numbered. For Twentyman, as for many of the town's inhabitants, the most significant event of this period following the second siege was the extension of the garrison's defences. By the time of the third and final siege they had been strengthened to such an extent that one contemporary observer described the town as having the appearance of a single impressive sconce. Twentyman provides a near contemporary account of the construction and appearance of some of these new defences and explains how they were manned. He pays particular attention to the activities of the town regiment in which his uncle was a captain. The extent and cost of these works are explored later in the book.[66]

And there was built a very noble and strong worke which the Townsmen
kept and built up an house of 3 or 4 Bay of Building in the middle of it, and
called it the Royall Sconse or else changed this name with that in my
close which in my time when it was made was called the king sconce
but it seemes was altered to the Royall Sconce, this new one takeing
the old name from it and because at Milngate End upon the south above
Markhall Bridge there was another very noble work called the Queen's sconse
The loyall Townsmen kept the king's sconce and were formed into a
Regiment. My uncle Edward Twentyman was the Eldest or first
Captain of that Regiment and died of a Gangrene which followed upon
butting of his Toe a little before the surrender of it.

In May 1644 the Royalist gains in Lincolnshire were reversed as the Earl of Manchester moved through the county with 6,000 men to join the siege of York. Both Lincoln and Gainsborough fell to his army and the Newark forces retreated to the vicinity of the town. Following the battle of Marston Moor, the Earl of Manchester returned to Lincoln and remained in the city for a month. During this period, despite having taken the Royalist garrison at Welbeck, he failed to use his advantage and attack Newark. He likewise eschewed the opportunity to reduce any of the small fortified outposts that surrounded the town - much to the consternation of his fellow officers, including Oliver Cromwell.

On 2 September 1644, the Parliamentarian army in the west under the command of the Earl of Essex surrendered to the Royalists at Lostwithiel and Manchester's forces were summoned south to offer greater protection to the capital. Newark was again spared and although the satellite garrisons at Crowland in Lincolnshire and

Thurgarton in Nottinghamshire were stormed in December 1644, the Newark horse was still free to collect the assessment from across much of Nottinghamshire. The account book of Gervase Hewet, treasurer to Colonel William Staunton's regiment at Newark, clearly shows that from December 1644 through to 20 April 1645 assessments continued to be collected from the villages allocated to the regiment. Soldiers travelled as far as Bunny in south Nottinghamshire and Selston in the north west of the county, both of which lay over 20 miles from Newark, during a period when local Parliamentarian forces were supposed to be closely policing travel into and out of the town.[67]

With the garrison at Newark strengthened by the flow of soldiers from the north, and the Earl of Manchester no longer in the vicinity after September 1644, the Royalists, with varying degrees of success, were able to initiate a number of raids. These included attacks on Sleaford, Gainsborough and Louth. At the end of October, however, the Royalists experienced a substantial defeat near Belvoir in Leicestershire. Encouraged by their success, Parliamentarians began to creep once again ever nearer to Newark. In early November they attacked Royalist regiments billeted at Farndon and East Stoke, capturing six officers and 85 troopers. These villages were within a mile or so of the town of Newark. Over the winter months, things became increasingly difficult for the town: though not actually besieged Newark was closely invested and everyday materials became increasingly scarce. Fortunately on the 25 February 1645, Sir Marmaduke Langdale and the Royalist Northern Horse defeated a small Parliamentarian force at Melton Mowbray in Leicestershire and were able to drop off provisions and munitions at Newark. Both the stores of the town and the spirits of its soldiers were replenished – at least for the time being.

One of the consequences of this series of setbacks was that Sir Richard Byron was dismissed as Governor of Newark in January 1645 and replaced by Sir Richard Willis.[68] The new Governor never obtained the wholesale support of Newark citizens and, indeed, appears to have earned the positive ire of Twentyman, who described him in his memoirs as 'a lewd and debauched person, [who] was corrupted by Oliver Cromwell'. Unlike his predecessor, Willis was an outsider with few links in Nottinghamshire. Both Byron and later Bellasis had estates in the vicinity of Newark and knew the area and its gentry reasonably well. Willis had none of these benefits and was generally viewed with suspicion – an opinion for which there may have been some foundation. Later in 1656, during the Republic, Willis became a double agent. He was a supporter of the Royalist Sealed Knot whilst at the same time supplied information to the Commonwealth authorities. In an undated letter he asked secretary Thurloe for a payment of £500 to act in this capacity and £500 more for revealing conspiracies against the Protector. After the Restoration, Willis was banned from the presence of Charles II for his double-dealings.[69] By the time Twentyman wrote his memoirs these details were public knowledge and they form part of his venomous attack on Willis.

On the 7 May 1645, Charles left Oxford with an army of 11,000 men with the intention of marching north to join the Earl of Montrose whose army was enjoying considerable success for the Royalist cause. As soon as he had left, Fairfax and the New Model Army besieged the Royalist headquarters at Oxford, forcing the king to change his plans and remain near to the town, should it be in need of relief. By the 28 May the king was at Loughborough, where he was joined by a further 1,200 horse from Newark under the command of Sir Richard Willis. Three days later, the king's army stormed the Parliamentarian town of Leicester, forcing Fairfax to end his siege of Oxford and come north to confront the king's army. After Leicester had been taken, Willis returned to Newark with 400 horse leaving the remainder of Newark's horse to travel on with the king. Fairfax and Charles' army met at Naseby on the 14 June and the result was a decisive victory for Parliament. The Newark horse fought on the left wing of the Royalist army as reserve to Sir Marmaduke Langdale's Northern horse. Both the Northern and Newark horse were thoroughly routed by the Parliamentarian horse under the command of Lieutenant General Oliver Cromwell. Some of the Newark horse managed to escape the carnage and on the 16 June a small group of them were ambushed in the vicinity of Leicester with 42 of their number being captured.[70] The king's main field was destroyed, with 4,000 prisoners being marched through London on the 21 June: the king's hopes for winning the war were shattered.

Following the defeat of the king at Naseby, Newark was initially spared a further Parliamentarian attack. Fairfax and the New Model Army were occupied in the southwest against Lord Goring's army, whilst the Scottish army was besieging

Hereford.[71] The garrison at Newark, now a rallying point for the broken forces of the Royalists, used this time to gather provisions, strengthen its defences and harass local Parliamentarian garrisons. On 16 July Newark forces retook Welbeck House and on 1 August 1645 they stormed Torksey House in Lincolnshire. Complaints poured up to Parliamentarian headquarters in London about the activities of the Newark horse and the authorities began to take note. On 4 October the king made his final visit to Newark with 1,400 men. He was again hoping to move northwards to join Montrose and his forces. (The news of Montrose's defeat at the battle of Philiphaugh, resulting in the destruction of the Royalist army in Scotland, had not yet reached the king). Whilst stationed in Newark the king found time to resolve a number of tensions existing within the garrison, not least a heated disagreement between Willis and the local commissioners of array. Indeed, one of Charles' last acts before leaving Newark for the final time was to replace Willis with Lord Bellasis as Governor of the garrison. Bellasis remained in command of Newark throughout the whole of the third siege and it was he who eventually surrendered the town.

The third and final siege of Newark began 26 November 1645 when the Scottish army under the Earl of Leven arrived to the northwest of the town and proceeded to occupy the Island. Although hostile forces were thus encompassing the town it was not until the end of March 1646 that it was closely invested. The plight of Newark was further aided by the harsh winter of 1645-1646, which considerably limited the actions of the Parliamentarians in the surrounding fields and villages. Surviving warrants and military orders show that the town had been well provisioned prior to the start of the siege,[72] and that conditions for the inhabitants - at the start of the siege - were not too harsh. For the besieging armies, by contrast, conditions were much worse, as the surrounding villages proved unable to supply either provisions or accommodation in sufficient quantity. On 13 December 1645 the London Militia Committee was ordered to provide fifty dragoons as a convoy for a provision train being sent to the forces around Newark. Even this additional assistance, however, failed to halt the flow of petitions from Nottinghamshire inhabitants complaining of the demands being made upon them by the besieging forces.

Newark's fate was finally decided not by military might but by the political machinations of Charles I. Throughout the early part of 1646, via the services of an agent of the French government, the king had been in communication with the Scots trying to come to some accord. By the end of April he had decided to risk all to gain the support of his former Scottish foes. Disguised as a clergyman and accompanied by two companions, the king arrived at Southwell on the 5 May and surrendered to the Scottish army besieging Newark. The alliance between Parliament and the Scots had begun to deteriorate owing to the former's prevarication over imposing a Presbyterian form of church government in England (as required by the Solemn League and Covenant). Charles hoped to exploit this tension by seeming to side with the Scots and appealing to their loyalty to the Crown. His hopes, however, were quickly dashed. The Scottish commander, General David Leslie, demanded that Charles order the immediate surrender of not only Newark but all Royalist garrisons. On receiving the royal command the Governor of Newark is alleged to have wept. The town mayor, meanwhile, suggested he ignore the order and sally out to do battle with the besiegers. In practical terms, however, Bellasis could not disobey the king's command, and so had no choice but to seek favourable terms for the surrender of the 'maiden garrison'.

Following the surrender the inhabitants of Newark fully expected that punishment for their loyalty to the king would result in wholesale plundering of the town. That it was not Twentyman attributed to the outbreak of plague which, he believed, discouraged the victorious besiegers from entering the town or remaining in the area. Other evidence suggests that it was not until late autumn – a number of months after the surrender on the 6 May - before the victorious Parliamentarians established a permanent garrison within the town.[73]

Newark had played a pivotal role throughout the course of the Civil War. Its soldiers and civilians experienced the consequences of war in all its many shades of brutality. Having explored the events of 1642-1646 in a narrative account, I will now proceed to analyse how these events impacted on the lives of ordinary people in the town. The economic, social, demographic and political repercussions of the war for the town will provide a focus for the rest of this book.

At the beginning of 1643 large sums of cash would have been quickly required to consolidate the garrison at Newark. Evidence from a later date suggests that this was achieved by taking up cash loans and the issuing of bonds by the Commissioners of Array. With the defeat of the Royalist cause in 1646, those who had lent money on bonds sought to retrieve what they could by taking legal actions against the commissioners. Whilst this action exposed them to financial penalties as 'delinquents' who had supported the king, it was hoped that they would regain at least some of their money. This action provides us with a valuable insight into sums of money involved and who was lending from within the town. An initial list of creditors drawn up on 29 December 1647 identified 47 individuals who were owed £11,170.19s.6d but this list was far from complete.[81] A number of individuals, because of their loyalty to the king, felt unable to involve themselves in legal proceedings and some of the creditors were commissioners who had been ordered to repay other outstanding debts.

A more detailed list of 1661 provides us with a clearer picture of the size of loans made and identifies a number of Newark's leading citizens who had loaned money. By 1661, the commissioners had repaid £11,285 to 35 individuals many of whom were aldermen who had served on the Borough Corporation of Newark. Three had served as mayor during the war, these being Mr Hercules Clay, Mr Christopher Wilson and Mr Alderman Baker. Also included on the list are a number of the town's merchants and also the vicar, Mr Trueman, who had served in the town during the war. Another £733 had still to be repaid 15 years on from the end of the war, whilst a further £2,479.15s.1d had been expended by individuals on provisions and munitions but not recompensed. In all, over £14,498.3s.2d was identified in this case alone and even by 1661 £3212.15s.1d had still not been repaid (see details below).

Figure 3.1 Loans made to the Royalist cause via the Commissioners of Array (1661)[82]

DEBTS UPON BOND WHICH ARE PAID

		£	s	d			£	s	d
To	Mr Barrett	£530	0	0	Brought Forward		£7564	0	0
	Mr Chambers	1500	0	0	Mr Bolles		150	0	0
	Mr Clay	636	0	0	Mr Trass		100	0	0
	Mr Trueman	320	0	0	Mr Camm		100	0	0
	Mr William Cooke	100	0	0	Earl of Scarsdale		1500	0	0
	Mr Newton	1000	0	0	Mr Stanhope		400	0	0
	Mr Alderman Johnson	840	0	0	Mr Zouch Wild		120	0	0
	Mr Christopher Wilson	200	0	0	Mr Rawson		40	0	0
	Mr Rooksby	200	0	0	Mr Alderman Wilson		100	0	0
	Messrs Stones & Fisher	200	0	0	Mr Robert Martin		31	0	0
	Mr Alderman Baker	156	0	0	Mr Alderman Standish		100	0	0
	Captain Hawley	132	0	0	Mr Peter Dickinson		136	0	0
	Mr Shipman	100	0	0	Mr Alderman Standish		51	0	0
	Mr Marshall	100	0	0	Mr Draper		650	0	0
	Mr Pasey	800	0	0	Mr Thomas Goodson		40	0	0
	Mr John Martin	100	0	0	Colonel Errington		100	0	0
	Mr Atkinson	600	0	0	Mr William Reason		53	0	0
	Mr Wilkinson	50	0	0	Mr Mason		50	0	0
	carry forward	£7564	0	0			£11,285	0	0

DEBTS UPON BONDS WHICH ARE NOT YET PAID viz. in 1661, Feb 14th

		£	s	d			£	s	d
To	Sir Guy Palmer	£200	0	0	Brought Forward		£588	0	0
	Sir Gervas Clifton	168	0	0	To	Mr Alderman Smith	70	0	0
	Sir Hugh Cartwright	200	0	0		Mr Alderman Hancks	75	0	0
	Mr Alderman Smith	20	0	0					
	Carry forward	£588	0	0			£733	0	0

The total of the debts upon bond as they were affixed to the petition presented to his Majesty Feb 14, 1661   £12,018.8s.1d

Debts contracted and acknowledged by the said commissioners which are yet unpaid and demanded by several persons, as followeth:-

		£	s	d		£	s	d
	Mr Langham demands	£150	0	0	Brought Forward	£270	0	0
	Hays the baker	40	0	0	Mr Brown	300	0	0
	John Hoyes	20	0	0	Mr Geo Cartwright	131	0	0
	Mr Palmer	60	0	0	Mr Nich Atkinson	200	0	0
	carry forward	£270	0	0		£901	0	0
The Lord Byron for several sums disbursed for the garrison						500	0	0
Sir John Digby for money disbursed by him about the powder mill						320	5	9
Sir Hugh Cartwright for arms delivered by him into the garrison						458	9	4
Sir Hugh Cartwright for corn delivered by him for the garrison						300	0	0
The Total of the debts without bonds but acknowledged and subscribed by all the commissioners to be due and unpaid						£2479.15.		1

Besides the great charges, not only in law suits about the said debts, but also in long imprisonment of some of the said commissioners who were sued for most of the said debts, both in chancery and at common law, they having been disabled to pay the same by reason of the sequestration upon their estates and their heavy compositions for them.

[Names underlined were residents of Newark prior to the outbreak of war in 1642]

Even before the bombardment endured by the town during its three sieges, the ruinous state of the domestic buildings at Newark Castle and the large numbers at the garrison made it necessary for the majority of soldiers to be quartered in people's homes. Both the town and its satellite villages would have accommodated soldiers and during those times when the Royalists enjoyed military ascendancy, communities even further a field would have had troops billeted on them. With the large numbers of cavalry based at Newark, this boarding outside the town would have been essential to provide fresh pasture for the horses. When there was cash available, the householder would have been paid for quartering soldiers. Each army had its standard rate of pay; in the New Model Army this ranged from 8d per day for a Trooper down to 6d per day for infantry, but details of the Newark garrison's rates have not survived.[83] During the latter part of 1644 the availability of cash diminished considerably and so the army often resorted to what was known as 'free quarter'. In these circumstances the householder was presented with a voucher instead of cash, which they were supposed to be able to redeem at a later date. It is not clear from surviving records how exactly this scheme was implemented and evidence suggests that often it did not work.

Little evidence survives about the process of quartering soldiers in Newark, but that which does certainly proves that soldiers were living in people's homes. The churchwarden's accounts for 1643-1644 record a payment of 2s.6d to a John Gill 'for a winding sheet and inkle for a soldier which died at his house'. Later after the siege of 1644 the accounts record the expenditure of 4s for two winding sheets for Prince Rupert's soldiers who died in the town several days after the military engagement.[84] An entry in the Corporation minutes for 1650 suggests that vouchers for quartering soldiers were not immediately redeemable. Francis Browne an alderman of the town was fined £10 for failing to fulfil his civic duties, possibly because of his disapproval of the recently declared Republic the previous year. The council allowed for the payment of the fine by 'some part in money, other part for quartering soldiers sent unto him by Mr Maior and the Aldermans appointed in those times of trouble'.[85]

A clearer picture of the effects of quartering soldiers upon a community is provided by the constable's accounts for the nearby village of Upton.[86] In 1644 the constables spent 1s.2d going to Newark to plead the village's case when 'Major Palmer would have quartered 30 men with us'.[87] Earlier in the year the sum of 10d had been expended on 'a souldier which did lie sicke at Kerkes for his lodgings & meat and drinke' whilst a few weeks later a further 4d had to be spent on providing a 'sacke for a Trooper which did lie sicke at John Kitchin his house'.[88] When officers were quartered in the village, further expenditure was required to entertain their guests. In 1645, 2s.6d was spent on 'tobaco and tobaco pippies for Captain Ashton when he quartered heare'.[89] If soldiers were not actually quartered in Upton then it was not uncommon for beds and bedding to be taken for them to sleep on at Newark. In August 1644, soldiers came to collect beds for the garrison, and again in 1645 'captain Chippindale soldiers....came for beds'. In the same year the villager John Chappell had to be paid by the parish 'for his fether bed that went to Newark', whilst in October the constable incurred expenses of 10d when he travelled 'with beddin to the Spittle Sconce'.[90] When soldiers were quartered in a house it was not uncommon for them to take anything of value from the householder. The wife of Thomas Kitchin was reimbursed 2s 'for a boulster', whilst Steven Shepherd's wife was paid 1s 'for a sheete' both of which were probably levied.[91] There is no reason to doubt that similar experiences befell the townsfolk of Newark, though their immediate proximity to the garrison commander possibly spared them the worst excesses of soldiers. During those times when Newark was closely invested by Parliamentarian forces, the full cost of quartering troops would have fallen on the town alone and after October 1645 there would have been little hope of alleviation.

The constant need of the Newark garrison to obtain gunpowder would also have a considerable impact upon the lives of ordinary citizens. In order to manufacture gunpowder a regular supply of one of its main constituents, potassium nitrate or 'saltpetre', had to be ensured. This was only available as a by-product of bird-droppings or human urine and its collection proved to be controversial. Prior to 1641 its collection had been a royal monopoly and 'saltpetre men' had a legal right to enter any house in the realm and dig in its hen houses or privies. The visit of such officials was both onerous and deeply resented. The Long Parliament had sought to curtail the activities of these 'saltpetre men' but the short supply of gunpowder during the war led to its re-imposition with renewed vigour.[92] In 1645 the constables of Upton spent 1s plying the saltpetre official with ale and then handed over a bribe of 5s.6d for the 'salt peeter man to goe from our towne'.[93] The citizens of Newark, being at the centre of gunpowder production for the area, would not have been able to rid themselves so easily of such officials.

Over the course of the war military reversals not only had strategic consequences for the garrison but also financial ones for the people of Newark. This is most clearly seen in the surviving evidence relating to the second siege of the town from 29 February to 21 March 1644. Newark was completely encircled and the Parliamentarians were able to bombard the town with both canon and mortar. As the situation deteriorated the governor, Sir Richard Byron, sent a message to the king pleading for assistance and relief. In his petition he highlighted how much money had been spent in establishing and maintaining the garrison.

> There has been expended by monies borrowed upon bonds by the gentlemen of both counties [Nottinghamshire and Lincolnshire] for the maintenance of his Majesty's forces and by assessment from the beginning of the war, a sum of at least £200,000.[94]

The longer the siege went on the greater became the need to secure cash both to pay the town's defenders and to strengthen its fortifications. The Corporation minutes for 1643-1644 listed townspeople who had lent money for the garrison's defence during 'the siege of this town began 29 February 1643(4)'.

Mr Thomas Hancke, maior	£5	William Smith	5s
William Martin	£5	Francis Browne	£10
Edward Newton	40s	Valentine Whitworth	40s
Mr Matthew Mercer	40s	William Barrett	£5
Mr Edward Standish	£5	Robert Gonison	£5
Widow Rogers	40s	Widow Middlebrooke	40s
John Sturtivant	£4	Robert Daintith	40s
William Watson	£5	John Marris	£10
John Martin	£5	George Welles	40s
Roger Whitton	40s		£75 5s toto[95]

Of the 19 individuals identified in this list, 12 failed to appear on the list of creditors issued in 1661.[96] Between them they lent £43.5s of the total and the fact that they did not appear on the 1661 list of creditors suggests that they were either dead by or, more likely, had not obtained bonds for the loan of their cash. Whatever the case, this additional levy suggests that the amounts of cash extracted from Newark's citizens was considerable and the Governor's estimate of money spent up to 1644 might not be as inflated as it first appears.

In the immediate aftermath of the second siege there was still further expenditure to be made. Prince Rupert's and Lord Loughborough's army remained at Newark until 27 March and his soldiers (and in particular his wounded) had to be quartered and cared for. The Borough Corporation also felt that due acknowledgement should be made to the Prince for his considerable military achievement in lifting the siege. The Chamberlain's accounts for 1644 recorded

> Paid to Mr Hancke, maior and by him disbursements to Prince
> Rupert's Trumpeters and servants at the raising of the siege as
> as appears by Bill £5 10s.[97]

Apart from such tantalising wisps of evidence such as these the relationship between military organisation and civilian affairs in Newark is especially difficult to gauge. The account for Colonel William Staunton's regiment of horse based at Newark provides us with some insights for a brief period from 1644 to 1645.[98] The accounts begin in the winter of 1644 when Parliamentarian forces under the command of Sir Edward Rossiter were in the area and were able to shadow the garrison's every move. They continue to record income and expenditure following Sir Marmaduke Langdale's victory at Melton Mowbray on 25 February 1645 (when there was a Royalist resurgence in the area) and finally peter out around the battle of Naseby. Throughout these fluctuations of fortune, the accounts clearly show that the regiment was able to collect the contributions allocated to it across several villages. The cost of supporting this locally raised regiment was not borne by the town of Newark alone but distributed across nine different parishes. These appear to have been allocated to the regiment not on the basis of geography but rather on their ability to pay. The parishes were spread over a wide area with its extremes being defined by Bradmore, (16 miles to the southwest of Newark) and Selston (21 miles to the west). The payment of soldiers' wages over this period accounted for over 60 per cent of the total regimental expenditure, whilst the purchase of horse fodder accounted for around 10 per cent (£34.16s.6d).

Some sections of Staunton's regiment were stationed at the village of Morton, but a sizeable portion was billeted at the Angel Inn in Newark, which was located on the west side of the Market Place. Senior officers, meanwhile, appear to have been accommodated at the Old White Hart Inn for an entry in the accounts recorded 'to my colonel at the Hart £2'. Whilst cash was being collected, the cost of accommodation was probably deducted from the soldiers' pay: the amounts paid, however, were probably less than the rates received from travellers during peacetime.

Cleaning and repairs to the stables, yard and surrounding streets were a financial responsibility carried by the regiment. Over the course of the war the amount of filth accumulated at the stables would have been considerable, as also would have been damage, and several entries in the accounts testify to this.

Jan.	10	For clenging ye yeard at ye Angell	2s
	10	For clenging ye street at wid. Teylers	2s
Mar.	28	To ye Qtr Master....& for ye repaireing of ye stables at ye Angell	5s
	30	For ye carpenters for repaireing of ye stable at ye Angell	13s.6d[99]

Whilst indigenous regiments appear to have joined with local citizens to shoulder cleaning responsibilities, when visiting armies were briefly quartered it was left to the Corporation to clean up after their departure. The chamberlain's accounts for 1644 record the payment of 6s 'for carriage away of dirt around the Horses house' and there are several payments recorded in the churchwarden accounts for cleaning away of dirt on or adjacent to church property.[100]

The town of Newark received several royal visits over the course of the war and a number of the peerage was also accommodated as they passed through. The hosting of such visitors and the quartering of their accompanying armies was another financial burden borne by the town and surrounding villages. A peel of bells heralded the arrival of Queen Henrietta Maria in June 1643 with the bell ringers receiving 5s for their performance. The Thorpe-by-Newark constables sent an additional £1.10s to the committee at Newark and spent a further 3s in conveying provisions of geese, turkeys, chickens and rabbits for the queen.[101] The constables at Upton spent 4d carrying provisions for the queen to Newark, but unfortunately the accounts do not identify what these were or their value. A further 3s was expended in trying to raise conscripts for the queen's army, as required by a warrant issued by the Commission of Array.[102] No records survive detailing what the townspeople of Newark supplied, but from the evidence of their neighbours it seems likely that it involved considerable expenditure. This is further suggested by a hospitality bill that has survived amongst the Borough's miscellaneous papers dated 5 January 1643(4) which noted the payment of £2.7s.8d in providing a banquet for

'Lord Withrington' during his visit. During the king's residence in the town during October 1645 another bill recorded a payment 'to ye sword bearer to ye king for his fees 6s.8d'.[103] On the 22 August 1645, the mayor Edward Standish handed over the sum of £5 on behalf of the Corporation as a gratuity to the servants of the king.[104] By this stage of the war the king's retinue was considerably reduced and the sum of £35 handed over in 1636 was unlikely to be repeated.[105] Very few bills survive from the Civil War period, but the few that managed to avoid destruction all suggest that considerable sums of additional money had to be spent by the town on nothing more productive than regal hospitality.

Within Newark, support for the king's cause amongst some residents went far beyond the payment of required levies and the quartering of soldiers. Towards the end of 1643 a small regiment of foot was raised from within the town. An order of payment dated 3 January 1644, issued by the mayor Thomas Hanckes and John and Edward Standish, survives amongst the miscellaneous papers of the Corporation instructing the chamberlain to hand over the sum of £1.19s.6d.

> For colours for the townsmen listed as soldiers for his
> Majesties service under ye command of Capt. Gervase Lee[106]

Gervase Lee of Norwell had a long record of service with the county's trained bands prior to the war, and in 1642 he had taken up arms for the king. According to evidence he gave to the Committee for Compounding in June 1646 he had to lay down his arms in 1643 due to ill health and infirmity.[107] Forced by the County Sheriff, Sir John Digby to retire into the Newark garrison it appears that the Corporation sought to use his expertise to train up their own regiment of townsmen. His son also appears to have come with him into the town for in 1645 he took charge of 60 musketeers from Newark who were sent to garrison Norwell.[108] No list of ordinary soldiers from Newark survives from this period and only those with estate worth over £200 had to compound with the victorious Parliamentarians after 1646. Many of the town's regiment were too poor to appear on this official list and so are lost to the historian. Edward Twentyman of Newark can be identified as either the senior or first active Captain of the regiment and a narrative containing the reminiscences of his nephew provides us with an extremely useful insight into life within Newark during these turbulent times.[109] His burial is recorded in the Newark registers on the 2 March 1646; thus he was spared the ignominy of the surrender in May of that year. Twentyman's will, however, may unwittingly provide us with an insight into other influential figures within the town regiment. In its preamble Twentyman describes himself as a 'gentleman' though his burial entry emphasises his military rank of Captain. The will notes that the 'present condicion of these tymes' might make the disposal of his 'body to the earth' difficult for his executors, possibly implying his fear that his death may occur whilst away on a military exercise. In fact he died in his chambers at the Saracen's Head Inn as a consequence of gangrene in his foot. It is the witnesses to his will, which are important, for they were probably close associates formed via his military activities. Two of the witnesses were clearly identified by the Parliamentarians as delinquents; Edward Standish (who was mayor in 1645 and adhered 'to the forces against Parliament') and John Martin whose occupation was given as a butcher but who 'voluntarily bore arms in the Newark garrison'. Martin appears to have readily slaughtered the plundered cattle for the garrison and may also have acted in a capacity as quartermaster for the town regiment.[110] The third witness was the town vicar Henry Trueman who probably served as the regiment's chaplain. Apart from bequests to his mother and brother, the only other individuals mentioned in Twentyman's will are the children of Thomas Treece, who was likewise identified as 'adhering to the king's side' and probably served in the town regiment.[111] Treece was also probably a cousin to Twentyman.

Other notable townsmen whose names appeared in the accounts of the Committee for Compounding and who most probably served in the town regiment were Edward Foster, John Conde, Richard Marshall, alderman John Norris, alderman William Watson, George Wood, Thomas Somers, Lancelot and William Thompson, Henry Gill, George Wells, William Baker and William Poulden. By 1649, Poulden had obtained the rank of Captain and was serving in the garrison at Pontefract during the second Civil War. Attempts by historians to identify his regiment during the first Civil War have not been successful and the reason for this may well lie in the fact that he served initially in the town's own regiment. He possibly received a commission in this service and rose to the rank of Captain on the death of Twentyman.

The town regiment served as a defence force for the garrison and, according to the Twentyman manuscript, was primarily responsible for the defence of the King's Sconce which lay to the north of the town and was probably constructed during

1644. The regiment was certainly active over the period 1644 to 1645 for the chamberlain's accounts recorded that the sum of £4.8s.9d was 'paid to Mr Newton for ribbon and match to the townes soldiers as appears by Bill and Warrant'.[112] The permanent strength of this regiment of townsmen is extremely difficult to estimate, but its main function of guarding the sconce and outworks would suggest a permanent strength of around a Company size (80-100 men). With rates of pay amounting to approximately 6d per day for a foot soldier and 8s. a day for a captain of foot, it is hard to envisage the Corporation incurring unnecessary expense when the demands of quarter and assessment from the garrison had also to be met.[113] So, during times of siege or attack, apprentices, shopkeepers, aldermen and their servants and others of the town's fit and able citizens would quickly arrive to strengthen this permanent core. According to Richard Franck at such times a force of 1,000 townspeople could be rallied.[114] Either this figure is an exaggeration or it suggests that youths and even women may have assisted in the defence. (In 1642, the population of Newark was only just over 2,000 and this, of course, included children). Evidence to suggest the inclusion of women and youths in the town regiment may be found in a Parliamentarian pamphlet of 1644 which recorded

> Yesterday, the Governor of Newark commanded all shops
> in the town to be shut, and all the townsmen to guard the works,
> most whereof are very willing.[115]

Such additional resources would have proved to be a tremendous asset to the Governor and his senior officers in defending the garrison and, at times, would have released garrison troops to mount military sallies against the besieging forces.

After the defeat of the king's main field army at Naseby on 14 June 1645 Royalist garrisons around the country began to negotiate for terms of surrender with Parliament. One of the consequences of this was that following the surrender of their own garrison, large numbers of soldiers were given permission to march to the nearest convenient Royalist stronghold, and for many this proved to be Newark. On 23 July 1645 the garrison at Scarborough surrendered to Parliament and some of its defenders were allowed to travel to Newark. Between 3rd and 24th August the Upton constables provided 'provisions for Skarborough men at Kelam' consisting of pigs, ducks, chickens, mutton and bread to the value of £2.18s.3d.[116] Later during the king's stay at Newark in October 1645, the constables provided a further £6 in cash to 'Sir Marmaduke Langdale's quarter master for provisions'.[117]

Generally, when a garrison surrendered it was the officers who moved on to other garrisons; ordinary soldiers tended to use the opportunity to return home or to re-enlist for the other side in the hope of gaining pay. At Newark the consequences of this were clearly displayed by the end of 1645. When Charles arrived at the garrison in October he found no fewer than 24 colonels and general officers resident in the town, each enjoying 'liberal assignments out of the contributions'.[118] Many of these officers had no regiments to command or only a small body of soldiers well below the strength generally required for such a rank. This placed a considerable financial burden on the local community and resulted in inadequate amounts of cash remaining to pay the ordinary soldiers.

Amongst the many new arrivals in Newark during the late summer of 1645 was at least one African who was described as a 'blackamoor'. He was possibly a slave to one of the Royalist officers (possibly even to the Earl of Newcastle who had black servants at Welbeck before the war) but he was most certainly a soldier in the garrison and his exploits were recalled as late as 1695 and told to Abraham de la Pryme. During one of the many sorties undertaken by the garrison during the final siege the 'blackamoor' soldier captured a Scottish soldier. In absolute terror, for he had never seen a black face before, the Scotsman exclaimed 'O God! O God! O God! Have mercy upon my sowl, the de'ils got my body'. He absolutely refused to go with his captor back into Newark and so eventually had to be killed.[119] His presence at the garrison is witnessed by a baptismal entry dated 30 March 1645, which recorded that a 'John Americanus, a blackamore' was christened.

By the end of 1645, cash had become extremely scarce within Newark and the growing Parliamentarian blockade exasperated the problem. In his diary the Royalist Sir Henry Slingsby recorded his own adventure in trying to remedy his lack of cash during the final siege at Newark. He wrote

> [going] in disguise from Newark to my own household with intention
> to supply my wants with money, whereof a long time I had had great
> scarcity....I went to my own house....after I had satisfy'd myself with
> one day's stay, and taken £40 in gold, I resolved to go back to Newark
> ....and as I came so I went, in disguise....and by good fortune return'd
> to Newark.[120]

To meet the urgent demand for coinage, a temporary mint was set up in Newark in 1646. Silver flagons, drinking cups, dishes and trenchers, often supplied by Royalist supporters within the town or deposited at the garrison for safe keeping by supporters in the surrounding areas, were fashioned into lozenge shape coins of values 2s.6d, 1s, 9d and 6d. Each siege coin had a specified weight of silver for its particular value; the 2s.6d was 128 grains whilst the 1s was 95 grains. The earliest coin was probably the 1s piece for some of them carry the date 1645 and in the old calendar the new year did not begin until 25 March (1646). Thomas Flower of Askham was one individual who smuggled plate into the town during this final siege and was summoned before Parliament's Committee for the Advancement of Money Causes to explain his actions.[121] For the town authorities too the supply of cash became a pressing issue. The chamberlain's accounts for 1644-1645 recorded an income of £72.6s but noted that rents to the value of £18.13s.2d could not be collected. The total expenditure for that year amounted to £94.9s.7d leaving a deficit of £22.3s.7d. The Magnus rentals for 1645 testify to even greater financial difficulties. Rents amounting to £77.4s.10d were collected but £76.8s.2d remained uncollected and the final account was in deficit to the sum of £28.8s.6d.[122] Around this time the corporation secured a loan of £100 from Widow Diana Gymney at an annual interest of 7 per cent to be paid in two half-year payments.[123] After the defeat at Naseby the collection of rents in north Nottinghamshire became almost impossible and by the time of its surrender in May 1646 the Newark Corporation was forced to sell a considerable amount of its remaining plate 'to supplie theire present want of money'. The list of items sold, but unfortunately not their weight or value, included

Thirteen Apostles Spoons	Twoe high Beere Bowles
Twoe Wine Bowles	One guilt wine Bowle
One great guilt Goblett	Five Trencher Salts
	One great Stooped Salt.[124]

Prior to the start of the third siege on 26 November 1645, there had been a concerted effort to secure provisions for the town and garrison. The king issued a warrant on 22 August 1645 instructing the governor Sir Richard Willis to bring corn into the garrison from the surrounding parishes and store it in the town. This, it was claimed, was to protect its owners from theft and they were to 'receive eyther satisfaction or have liberty to dispose it'.[125] As the siege went through the long hard winter of 1645/46, the quality of provisions deteriorated considerably and the efficiency of the besieging army meant that no new provisions got through. Whilst there was no question of starvation, the quality of food for both civilian and soldier was very poor. A parliamentarian tract of 1646 observed the effects of poor food and lack of money upon the relationship between town and garrison, which prior to the final siege, had been generally good.

> There hath lately been in Newark great contestation between Bellasis, the Governor, and the king's commissioners there, and the officers and soldiers for pay and provisions. The Governor told the commissioners that his soldiers wanted money, but they professed that there was none for them to be had; but they told him that for provisions he might dispose unto them what quantities he pleased. Bellasis replied that soldiers must and should have monies whilst any of them had a farthing, and that for the provisions in the magazine he told the commissioners that the greatest part thereof was such as no dogge would eat, and therefore charged them to bring forth better, or else he and his soldiers would rifle their houses and take their provisions they had stored up for themselves, and leave them the rotton stuff in the magazine to feed upon; and he further told them that they were not to expect that he and his soldiers would fight to preserve them and their town without those things should presently be remedied, and that for his part he said he did know well how to make honourable and good conditions for himself, his officers, and soldiers, and would leave them and the townsmen to shift for themselves if they took not care for them.[126]

Evidence from within the garrison does not suggest that tensions were as great as this piece of Parliamentarian propaganda suggests, but there can be little doubt that conditions became increasingly harsh. Certainly, poor diet contributed to the high mortality rates that both typhus and plague wrought in the town over this period. At the surrender of the garrison in May 1646 there remained considerable ammunition, but few provisions: 'little fresh meat', salted meat but 'much of it tainted'; some stores of butter and cheese, many barrels of beer and wine, a good store of corn; 'but fewel for fire very little'.[127]

The surrender of the garrison in May 1646 brought little by way of relief for the citizens of Newark from either economic hardship or dearth. The fact that the plague was raging in the town at its capitulation probably spared it from immediate occupation by the victorious besiegers, and it was not until November 1646 that the town was deemed safe enough for Parliamentarian soldiers to be stationed there. A hospitality voucher in the corporation papers records the expenditure of 2s.6d on 20 November and a further 2s.4d on 26 November for 'sugar nutts and tobacco for Colonell Thornhaugh at Mr Bakers, maior'.[128] Francis Thornhagh of Nottingham was Colonel of the Nottinghamshire Horse until his death during the battle of Preston in August 1648. A receipt, which survives from 1647, gives us some idea of the tremendous expenses incurred by the Newark townspeople in supporting this Parliamentarian occupation and policing of their town following the Civil War.

Arrears due ye soldiers 21 June 1647 from Corporal Meares

For 20 soldiers pay for 3 weeks at 10s a man	£30.00
For 9 weeks pay of 10 soldiers at Xs a man	
beginning 8 March 1646(7)	£45.00
	£75.00 [129]

This expenditure for a three month period exceeded that spent on poor relief for the whole of 1645 and was just below the annual rental amount received from the Magnus charity lands (£77.4s.10d) in the same year. The ending of the war did little to ease the financial burden for the citizens of Newark and appears to have continued right up until the end of the 1640s.

The years 1647-1649 witnessed a succession of bad harvests resulting in a dearth of grain, escalating prices and further hardship for the people of Newark.[130] In an attempt to mitigate the consequences, the Borough Corporation passed a series of measures the first of which was recorded on 2 December 1647. Noting that the 'sellinge of corne and graine in private places of this towne, out of the publique market is found to be very mischievous (especially in this time of scarcitie) tendinge to the inhancement of prices thereof' the Corporation ordered that all corn was to be 'openlie sold in the market' only after the ringing of the market bell. They further ordered that 'noe inhabitant suffer corne to be sett or sold in their houses' and that a fine of 20s was to be imposed for every such offence.[131] In spite of these measures prices continued to rise and hunger became an increasing reality for the poorer members of the town. By February 1649 conditions were so difficult that further orders were issued.

That noe maulster or badger whatsoever shall or dureing this time
of scarcitie buy any Barley within this towne or market to convert
the same into mault upon paine to be preceded against in the Sessions
of the Peace within this town.[132]

Despite the hardships, no evidence survives to suggest that there were either riots or any form of public disorder as a consequence of this dearth of grain. It may be that the close policing of this former Royalist town by the victorious Parliamentarians made such actions extremely difficult. Only with the return of better harvests after 1651 was this situation reversed and an improvement of conditions experienced within Newark.

Destruction of Property

By 1642 the medieval town walls of Newark were obsolete and in a number of places partly destroyed. The town had long spread beyond them in ribbon development along both North Gate and Mill Gate.[133] The latter was an important centre for the town because of the corn and fulling mills, which were located there. Along with Barnby Gate and Balderton Gate, Mill Gate also contained numerous domestic buildings.[134] The flow of traffic into and out of the town was channelled through the medieval town gates on Bar Gate, Castle Gate and Bridge Street, which still survived. On market days these routes would have witnessed considerable congestion. The town itself consisted predominantly of timber-framed buildings with only a few stone structures. The castle was still habitable, though many of its buildings were in a ruinous state. During the Civil War the majority of the garrison would have to be billeted around the town in inns and private houses. The spire of St. Mary's church was the most prominent feature on the skyline, visible for many miles around. Outside the old walls stood the recently built stone house of the Earl of Exeter that was situated on the site of the Spittal, an old medieval 'hospital' being demolished to allow its construction.

The preponderance of timber-frame buildings meant that fire was always a danger, even in more peaceful times. The Corporation constantly monitored the provision and condition of the town's fire-fighting equipment, which was ordered to be stored at St. Mary's church. An inventory of the equipment in 1629 listed 'three draggs, twelve buckets and a pole to pull them downe'. By 1661, this had increased to 21 buckets, six ladders and three draggs, even though the number of houses in the town was considerably reduced.[135] The experience of bombardment and siege during the 1640s had raised the spectre of fire in such a way that the Corporation closely supervised the provision of equipment for many years to come. In many towns the inhabitants were required to place tubs of water outside their homes in case of fire, though there is no evidence of this being enforced in Newark: close proximity to the rivers Trent and Devon to the town probably made this provision less necessary.

With the outbreak of hostilities in the autumn of 1642, Newark, with its ruinous medieval defences and inadequate fire-fighting provision, proved to be ill-prepared for military conflict. By the winter of 1643 a basic earthen defensive circuit had been hastily erected around the old town, which also took in a small part of North Gate and Mill Gate.[136] John Twentyman, described these initial works as 'very low and thin with a dry ditch which most men might easily jump'.[137] Such defences, however, whilst causing a degree of inconvenience for the town's inhabitants, probably required little destruction of property. That they gave little protection during the first siege is evident as Parliamentarian artillery situated on Beacon Hill bombarded Newark and fighting raged within the town right up to the base of the hurriedly erected defences. Although the siege was quickly repulsed, damage had been inflicted on a number of Newark properties, and the Governor had learnt a useful lesson. Extensive demolitions of property to build new defences and provide clear fields of fire quickly followed.

Military manuals of the sixteenth and seventeenth century taught that the clearance of property in the suburbs or close to a town's defensive perimeter was essential for garrison security.[138] Often these buildings were constructed of a timber frame with a lath and plaster filling and a thatch roof, which made their dismantling or destruction a relatively simple matter. After the first siege of 1643, the domestic buildings outside Newark's defences in North Gate were recognised as providing possible cover for future attacks. According to Thoroton, 'Sir John Henderson, the prudent Governor, caused all Northgate and the forementioned House [Exeter House] to be burned'.[139] There appears to have been little thought given to moving these buildings, as had happened in other towns': rather they were simply put to the torch. The cost of incorporating this elongated ribbon development of Newark into the Civil War defences was so high, both in terms of labour and finance, that it proved easier to destroy them.

The summary way in which the Governor's instructions were carried out is a testimony both to the insubstantial nature of these buildings and the very real fears that possessed the military authorities. Not all the buildings were completely destroyed however. Exeter House, or the Spittal, was constructed of stone and failure to demolish the walls after the fire meant that 'the case of it made a receptacle for the enemy at the second siege'.[140] Apart from the incidence of Exeter House, the surviving Corporation records fail to provide any evidence about the general scale of destruction, its costs, or the thorny issue of compensation. In fact, they fail to mention the event at all. The accounts of the Overseers of the Poor have not survived and so it proves very difficult to gauge the impact of this action upon its victims. This lack of reference to the event in the town's records may suggest that it was dealt with as a purely military matter with the Governor dealing directly with the financial implications of the act. Even if this was the case and some form of financial compensation was provided, land for rebuilding within the defences was severely limited and the consequence would have been increased overcrowding. This would have severe repercussions for sanitation and the health of the population.[141]

In the months following the lifting of the first siege in 1643, new defences were also erected for according to Twentyman 'at this time they also secured the street called Miln [sic] Gate'.[142] Earthworks were also raised to protect the bridge at North Gate and also to strengthen the approach to Appleton Gate. Amongst a collection of hospitality vouchers in the Borough records is a receipt dated January 1644 for £10 'layd out for ye works in Appleton'.[143] This erection of new defensive works at Newark continued right up until the third and final siege of 1645-1646, and would have necessitated the destruction of further property. Bastions, forts, wide ditches and sconces all occupied more land than the simpler Medieval defences and by the end of the war such works were extensive both in and around Newark, being built by both besiegers and besieged. Because new earthworks were faced with turf to give them greater resilience against canon balls and protect them from erosion, surrounding pasture land may also have been adversely affected.[144]

The second siege of Newark began on 29 February 1644 when Sir John Meldrum invested Newark with an army of 7,000. He also brought with him 11 cannons and two mortars, which according to Twentyman bombarded the town both day and night. The mortars proved to be especially lethal to property as they launched explosive grenades into the town from the nearby Beacon Hill. A grenade exploding amongst densely packed timber buildings and thatch had the potential to do much damage and possibly cause a firestorm. To the civilian population of Newark the mortar grenades were probably more frightening than cannon shot because they could affect a much larger area.[145] The fact that Newark was bombarded in the winter months, at all three sieges, when both timber and thatch were wet probably spared the town from a major fire. Amongst the buildings destroyed by mortar grenades was the house of the Mayor of Newark, Hercules Clay, which stood in the Market Place. After a series of dreams, Clay had moved his family out of the house the day before it was hit and in thankfulness that 'it pleased God of his infinite mercy wonderfully to p[re]serve me and my wife from a fearefull destruction by a terrible blowe of grenadoe...' he left in his will £100 to the poor and a further £100 for a sermon to be preached annually on 11 March - the anniversary of his deliverance.[146] An insight into what such destruction could mean for the poorer members of society is provided by the chance survival of a petition presented by Charles Piggot. Although undated, it almost certainly originates from the period following the second siege because the reverse side of the parchment was used to write the will of Thomas Waite, which was made on 20 July 1644. The proving of this will guaranteed the survival of the petition. Piggot pleaded

> Your poore peticioner hath in a verie large manner tasted of the
> miseries and affliccons of these tymes for at the last fight against
> Newarke he had his house blowne upp with a granado and all his
> goods burnt and broken to the utter undoeinge of your poore
> peticioner, his wife and seaven children.[147]

He goes on to petition Sir John Digby, the former Sheriff and now based at Newark garrison, for 'some allowance towards the buildinge of the said house and furnishing of it againe'. Piggot seems to have had some support from the town in this appeal for the hand that wrote his petition also penned a number of the townspeople's wills at this time and such service would have cost money. The outcome of the request is unrecorded, but the family's financial situation continued to remain precarious. By 1664, Piggot was living in a one hearth dwelling in Mill Gate but was so poor that he was exempt from the payment of hearth tax.

The bombardment of the town over the three weeks of the second siege probably caused considerable damage to a number of properties but little evidence remains to detail this. Cannon shot fell on the house of Alderman Baker (Mayor of the town in 1646) and also on the home of Mr Christopher Wilson (Mayor in 1655), their social status within the town guaranteeing the marking of such events.[148] A cannon ball is claimed to have passed through the steeple of St. Mary's but caused no damage to the church, although a hole is still visible today. The town appears to have been spared any major catastrophes during its numerous bombardments. A military garrison normally meant the establishment of magazines of match, gunpowder and other combustible materials. A powder mill was also established at Mill Gate and there survives warrants for the moving of gunpowder from Newark to the surrounding garrisons.[149] Had any of these stores or workshops been hit by artillery fire then both the damage and the number of casualties within the town would have been considerably greater. With the lifting of the siege by Prince Rupert on the 22 March, renewed efforts were made to repair damage and strengthen the towns defences, especially after the defeat of the king's Northern army at Marston Moor.

It was not only domestic buildings that were damaged during the first two sieges; a number of the town's public buildings including the church were also affected. Prominent on the skyline, St. Mary's church was always a vulnerable building. Following the skirmish and siege of 1643, £2.9s.4d had to be spent by the wardens on repairs to the lead roof and 10s.6d on the windows. Under Laudian pressure to 'beautify churches' during the latter part of the1630s, Newark churchwardens had spent £13.17s.10d on restoring the church windows and repairing over 400 holes in the glass in 1640.[150] The subsequent damage to the windows over the course of the Civil War would have been particularly galling to the church officers. The military activities of the second siege were much more pronounced, including artillery bombardment of the town, and so it is not surprising to find extensive repairs being undertaken on the church. By the early summer of 1644, £1.14s.2d had been spent on roof repairs whilst with the onset of winter a further £2.6s was expended on the church windows. By April 1645 a further sum of £2.7s had been disbursed on the windows after additional monies had been raised. During the same month restoration of the stonework and 'battlements' of the church was undertaken at a cost of £1.10d. This work may have included repairs to the steeple, which had been damaged by cannon fire in 1644. An interesting entry in the churchwarden accounts notes 'the carriage of a stone from Northgate'.[151] It is possible that stone from the now demolished Exeter House was being used within the town for repairs, mainly to military defences but some perhaps being allocated to the church.

At a time when the financial burdens of maintaining the military garrison at Newark fell particularly heavily on the townspeople, these additional expenses would have been extremely irksome. When the wardens required additional monies, they raised them by the collection of 'lays' or 'leys', being an additional quarter's assessment upon all eligible inhabitants. An additional lay of this kind was collected in three successive years, from 1643 to 1645 (5 quarter assessments per annum). Although over £4 was spent on repairs to the church roof over these three years, it appears that the church kept its roof and did not have it stripped by the military garrison for conversion into lead bullets. The church, however, may not have been so fortunate during the third and final siege of 1645-46 (see below).

In 1645, the Corporation also had to spend the sum of 10s.8d on repairs to the Market Cross, which also may have been damaged during the siege of the previous year.[152] Other buildings would most certainly have been damaged but unfortunately no accounts survive to detail these.

Following the defeat of the king's field army at Naseby on 14 June 1645, Newark became increasingly isolated as the only significant Royalist garrison in the north. Realising that time was limited before an assault was launched, the Governor, John Bellasis, began to prepare the town for the forthcoming storm. Maintenance of Newark's defences had been ongoing throughout the war but in the final months of 1645 work increased considerably and new defensive works were added. These included a high rampart and ditch around the town, interspersed with several forts each within musket-shot of one another. Two large sconce forts were also erected to the north and south of the defences; the so-called King's and Queen's Sconces. Properties that compromised the defences of the town were also demolished or removed, depending upon the social status of its owner and the type of dwelling. Surviving in the Corporation minute book is an order issued on the 23 September 1645 to the executor of the will of Thomas Waite instructing him to dismantle a tenement, which possibly interfered with the town defences.

> Whereas there is a small tenement consisting of two bayes of building
> lately erected upon the townes land at Milngate and nere the river of
> Trent by Thomas Waite deceased, w[hi]ch said tenem[en]t is by order
> of the Generall and Comissioners appointed to be taken downe for the
> strengthening and better fortifieing of the Bulworks there....and the same

to reedifie upon some part of the ground belonging to the Corporacon, soe
soone as the same may or can be done with conveniency.[153]

The less substantial dwellings of the town's poorer residents may well have been demolished with less care or thought and so they fail to appear in the surviving records.

The start of the third and final siege of Newark is dated to the arrival of the Scots army to the north of the town on 26 November 1645. It was not until the completion of their two lines of circumvallation in March 1646 that the town was completely invested. Over the six months of the siege, the Scots and English Parliamentarian armies pounded the town with shell and shot. A letter to William Lenthal, Speaker of the House of Commons, noted

the field officers have viewed the most convenient places for
forts to shoot either into the town or sconces, which are in
preparation, and will speedily be finished.[154]

The besiegers used a number of artillery pieces; Richard Clampe's map of the siegeworks (1646) shows at least 23 cannons around the line of circumvallation. Correspondence dated the 18 March 1646, meanwhile, records that 'the cannon from York has come to Winthorpe...[and] culverins and mortar pieces are come to Balderton and Farndon'.[155] Not all their artillery fire proved to be effective against the town, however. A contemporary account noted

the enemy within doe begin to be much distracted, and the rather
because our mortar piece doth already begin to play upon them,
although at first with greater fright than execution, because
it is said that firemen could not finde the ground[156]

Constant bombardment over the six months of the siege would have caused considerable damage within the town. Parliamentarian news sheets recorded that there were 'thatcht houses and ricks of Hey and corne' and that 'divers houses [were] burnt and battered downe' by their artillery.[157] By early spring 1646, fire would have been a very real concern for the inhabitants of Newark. The besieging forces under the command of General Poyntz had built a dam on the river Devon and had begun to dam the Newark arm of the river Trent in an attempt to deprive the town's mills of water. A reduction in the water level of the town's rivers would have made the task of extinguishing fires begun much more difficult. The lack of surviving records makes a detailed analysis of property destruction impossible, but there seems little doubt that living conditions would have been extremely unpleasant for its citizens. The impact of the bombardment would also have frustrated efforts to quarantine the plague then raging in the town.

Extensive damage was inflicted upon the parish church of St. Mary's during this final siege. Masons were paid the sum of 6d on 21 April 1646 'for gathering up ye Pinacles, lead and glasse battered downe in ye siege' and 5s.6d was laid out on the endless task of repairing the windows. Major repairs could not be initiated though until after the garrison's surrender and the plague had subsided. By the beginning of December 1646, the large sum of £7.15s.6d had been spent on major repairs to the church roof. Within 18 months of this a further £4.6s.7d was disbursed on the 'leads and spouts' of the church. The amount of lead purchased over this period may suggest that, towards the end of the siege the Royalist garrison stripped off part of the roof to make bullets for their muskets. Before the surrender of the town money was also out laid on moving some of the church furnishings and fittings into hiding so as to avoid their destruction.[158]

On the Restoration of Charles II in 1660, the town of Newark sought to extract a renewal of its Charter, as a reward for loyal service to the Crown during the Civil War. With their petition of 1661 they enclosed a résumé of damage and costs incurred by the town during the conflict. According to the petitioners the sum of £40,000 was lost

> by the burning of a sixth part of the town when it was made a garrison,
> by erection of works, moneys lent and never repaid, (and) quartering
> of soldiers.[159]

Whilst this final figure may have been slightly exaggerated to add weight to the petition (the passing years may have aided this process of embellishment) there was most certainly extensive damage inflicted upon the town during the three sieges. The ability of individuals to rebuild their damaged or destroyed properties once the fighting had ceased was considerably impaired by other financial losses experienced during the war. Numerous individuals in Newark were identified by the victorious

Parliamentarians as 'delinquents' and so were forced to pay fines or 'compositions' to retain what remained of their estates. The impact of plague, meanwhile, meant that trade and commerce were greatly curtailed for several months after the surrender of the town. With little coinage available, rebuilding would have been delayed for many individuals.

As late as 1664, of the 516 households listed in the hearth tax returns only 244 (just over 47 per cent) were eligible to pay the levy. Many people were still living in unsubstantial or damaged dwellings and, as a result of their impoverishment, were exempt from the tax. By 1672 conditions in the town appear to have improved for by then 379 were liable to pay the assessment.[160] Where the damaged or destroyed property had been leased, disagreements between landlord and tenant over responsibility for repairs could further delay rebuilding. A court ruling of 1646 in the case of Paradine versus Jane, ruled that rent must continue to be paid on damaged properties 'as the Lessee is to have the advantage of casual profits, so he must run the hazard of casual losses, and not lay the whole burthen of them upon his Lessor'.[161] Lack of finance meant that many leased properties remained in a ruinous state for many years. Poorer tenants experienced considerable hardship and discomfort and were probably under constant harassment from landlords to repair their damaged dwellings. The cost of erecting new buildings ranged from around £10 (or even less for the humblest of dwellings) to around £40 for a timber-framed house, and £60-80 for the average stone built town house.[162] For many of Newark's inhabitants this sort of expenditure was just not possible in the aftermath war. Thus, the repair and rebuilding Newark's damaged properties was a long, drawn-out affair, which extended throughout the 1650s and into the early 1660s.

CHAPTER 4

"A miserable, stinking, infected town':
Pestilence, plague and death, 1640-1649

To the early modern mind, the association of soldiers and warfare with the spread of typhus, plague and other epidemic diseases was long established. Typhus or 'camp fever' had first been noted in Europe at the end of the fifteenth century and Girolamo Fracastoro wrote the first substantial medical treatise on it in 1546[163]. By 1643 Lady Fanshawe was able to observe and comment during the siege of Oxford

> at the windows the sad spectacle of war, sometimes plague,
> sometimes sicknesses of other kinds, by reason of so many
> people packed together.[164]

For the civilians of Newark, disease and death were to be an ever-present reality throughout the period of the first Civil War. As this chapter will show, disease (particularly typhus and plague) were to kill more of the local population than the fighting ever did. From 1643 to 1645, typhus the occupational disease of armies and an inevitable consequence of the Civil War, surfaced with lethal regularity over the winter months. This disease was quickly communicated to civilian populations whenever towns were placed under siege, or when troops were billeted in them. Several Royalist armies from outside the region were to be accommodated in or around the town throughout the war and in 1645-46 two armies, the English Northern Association Army and the Scottish Army of the Solemn League and Covenant, invested the garrison right up to Newark's outer defences. The deprivation, filth and sheer volume of people concentrated in such a small area, proved to be catalysts for the spread of disease.

Over the last four decades, local and regional studies of the Civil War have enabled us to assess the social and economic impact of fighting upon communities. An assessment of the demographic consequences of the war and the interaction between military and civilian mortality rates has proven much more difficult to ascertain because of the fragmentary nature of surviving evidence. In the face of epidemic or in the aftermath of fighting recording each death in the parish registers could be overlooked and military casualties were often buried where they fell or in plots away from the churchyard.[165] In the face of such social disruption, the fact that an attempt was made to maintain the registers at all bears testimony to the resilience of community life. The town of Newark remained a Royalist garrison throughout the whole of the first Civil War and this facilitated the maintaining of its civic and ecclesiastical records for most of that period. Although many of its military records were possibly destroyed before the surrender of the garrison (in an effort to avoid recriminations) there remains enough evidence to add considerably to the ongoing debate about the demographic impact of the Civil War. As will be shown, this evidence serves to clarify many questions that remain unanswered, as well as provide insight into areas about which previous historians could offer little more than hints.

A clearer picture of just how devastating the experience of war was may be obtained by examining the mortality rates for Newark over the four decades leading up to 1642. Newark had never been a particularly healthy place to live in for the majority of its citizens. Situated alongside the river Trent, with its associated problems of flooding and water-borne infections, and with its narrow, overcrowded alleys and areas of poor quality housing, Newark was always susceptible to outbreaks of disease, which affected both young and old. The size of the town's population in the seventeenth century has proved difficult to assess with any degree of accuracy. Based on the figure of 70 burials that occurred over the year 1599-1600, A. C. Wood has suggested that, at the beginning of the century, Newark had a population of over 2,000.[166] Later work on the hearth tax returns of 1674 has estimated a population of around 1,444, but this low figure probably reflects an under-recording of households by about 25 per cent. Estimates based on parish register data have suggested a population of 2,774, but the multiplier used is now generally regarded as too high.[167] For our period of 1640-1660, a round figure of 2,000 for the town's population does not contrast greatly with the various estimates arrived at from the different sources and provides us with a solid basis from which to interpret the trends identified in the parish registers. The various estimates paint a picture of a population that was generally static for most of the century and may even have declined slightly. As we shall see, the traumatic events of the 1640s and 1650s may have contributed to this decline.

Table 4.1 Pre-civil war mortality figures for Newark

Period	Number of years	Total funerals	Annual mean	Total adults deaths	Adult annual mean	Total child deaths	Children annual mean
1600-1603[1]	4	373	93.25	186	46.5	187	46.75
1621-1625	5	465	93	260	52	205	41
1626-1630	5	431	86.2	256	51.2	175	35
1631-1635	5	445	89	420	84	[25][2]	[5]
1636-1640	5	451	90.2	289	57.8	162	32.4

(1) Only incomplete burial records survive from 1604-1609, but for this four-year period the age of every person over one year old is recorded in the register. This makes the distinction between children (under 16) and adults very clear.

(2) Details distinguishing adult from child burials are not accurately recorded for this period. Full family reconstruction would be required to clarify this which is beyond the scope of this book.

Table 4.1 provides us with mean burial totals at Newark for five-year periods in the two decades leading up to the Civil Wars, and also for the first four years of the century. The overall picture conveyed by these figures is of a burial average that did not greatly deviate from around 90 per annum for most of this period. There does appear to have been a slight improvement between the high rate of 93.25 at the start of the century and the figure of 86.2 by the end of the 1620s. Yet, during the 1630s average burial rates began to rise again and the years 1639 and 1640 witnessed a considerable rise (see Table 4.2).

Table 4.2 Annual burial data used for Table 4.1

Year	adult	child	Year	adult	child	Year	adult	child	Year	adult	child
1600	45	35	1623	63	47	1629	40	46	1635	88	5
1601	39	45	1624	57	24	1630	60	45	1636	50	24
1602	75	74	1625	68	34	1631	83	16	1637	47	21
1603	27	33	1626	60	21	1632	71	1	1638	58	33
1621	28	48	1627	49	26	1633	81	2	1639	72	32
1622	44	52	1628	47	37	1634	97	1	1640	62	52

The general trend for child burials over the period 1600-1640 is clearly one of improvement with the mean falling from 46.75 down to 32.4. The reason for this is unclear but it is possible that improved conditions within the town led to this fall. In 1640, however, this trend was brought to a sudden halt with 52 children being buried; a harbinger of the lean years that lay ahead. A note of caution must be acknowledged at this point. Parish registers list burials in the churchyard only and do not record deaths in the parish in general. As a result, they are particularly liable to understate the extent of mortality during an epidemic or time of war. Even so, what the registers do record in the 1640s clearly demonstrates that the town was experiencing considerable demographic disruption.

Following the initial battle of the Civil War at Edgehill in October 1642, there was a renewed impetus on both sides to secure and garrison key towns across the country. In December 1642, the Earl of Newcastle sent around 4,000 Horse to help secure Newark for the king and by the time they withdraw in January 1643 the town had a well-established garrison.[168] A muster of local troops held in May of that year showed that by then around 2,000 soldiers were permanently stationed in and around the town.[169] As the war progressed, this number would increase substantially as Royalist armies led by Queen Henrietta Maria, Prince Rupert and the king himself were occasionally billeted in the town as they passed through on their travels. When the town finally surrendered in May 1646, after much deprivation and disease, between 1500 and 1800 soldiers were allowed to march out by the Parliamentarians and Scots. A large proportion of the garrison at Newark consisted of cavalry and the Newark horse achieved considerable local notoriety. The horses had to be stabled in the town or at neighbouring villages but during times of siege - and more permanently after November 1645 - they would have had to be brought into the defensive network around the town. Field officers probably kept their horse in the town throughout the war. The account book for the regiment of Colonel Staunton kept by Lieutenant Gervase Hewet clearly shows this to be the case. In 1645 he records both the payment of 13s.6d 'to ye carpenters for repaireing ye stables at ye Angell' and the expenditure of 2s 'for clenging ye yeard at ye Angell'.[170] Other payments were made for stabling within the town but for Staunton's regiment the Angel Inn appears to have been their base. The parish registers also suggest that a number of officers and men brought their families with them into the garrison. Both children and other family members occasionally appear in the christening or burial lists for this period. Neighbouring gentry and clergy with known Royalist sympathies also appear to have moved both their families and some of their possessions into the town for safekeeping.

As a result of this garrisoning of the town the population of Newark would have at least doubled for the duration of the war and there would have been brief periods when it might even have trebled. Yet at the very time when more people were pouring into the town, the amount of accommodation for them to occupy was being reduced. Houses and tenements that abutted the defensive perimeter had been pulled down and new building was carefully controlled by the Borough Corporation.[171] The consequence of this was considerable overcrowding and an increase in filth and congestion. This sheer mass of humanity crowded into a small area and exposed to the deprivations of war proved ripe for the ravages of disease. The fact that troops were also occasionally stationed in surrounding villages also meant that disease was carried out of the town into these rural communities.

The main epidemic disease that periodically afflicted Newark throughout much of the war was typhus, an ailment directly associated with the movement of troops. Typhus is carried by human body lice. Its classic symptoms include fever leading to a stupor with extraordinary headaches and red pustules resembling fleabites over the body of the sufferer. Epidemics usually began at the start of the winter months when the cold weather discouraged bathing and the changing of clothes. Such conditions were ideal for body lice to thrive and typhus proved to be the scourge of field armies throughout the ages.[172] Whilst potentially lethal for adults, typhus rarely killed children; although they sickened from the disease, their mortality rate remained low. In Newark's burial registers there are noticeable occasions where there is a preponderance of adult deaths over children and this often coincides with the aftermath of substantial military action.[173] The winters of 1644 and 1645 were also extremely harsh with the river Trent freezing and floating ice causing damage to the town's wooden bridges.

These factors, coupled with increased malnutrition amongst the civilian population were all conducive to the spread of typhus.

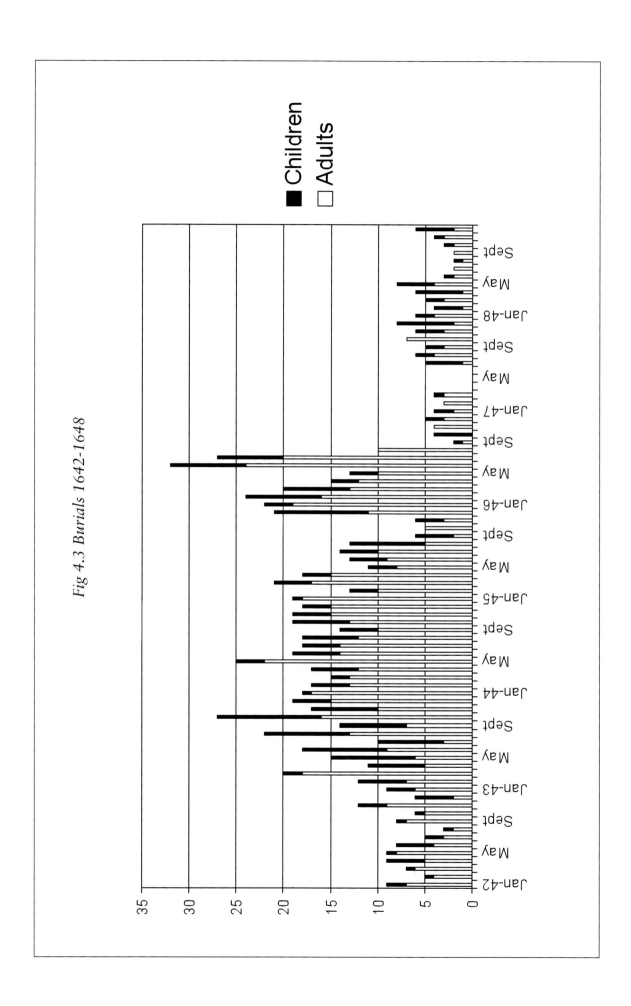

Fig 4.3 Burials 1642-1648

The first major outbreak of typhus in the town followed the first siege between 27 and 28 February 1643 (see fig 4.4). In March the number of burials rose by over 66 per cent from 12 to 20. Only one of these burials was of a soldier, a Captain John South, and children only accounted for two of the total. This was considerably less than the 5 infant burials in February and the 6 in April. The rest of the casualties were civilians and the registers make no reference to them being casualties from the previous month's conflict.

The winter of 1643-1644 also proved to be a traumatic time for the citizens of Newark. In October 27 burials were recorded, a monthly figure not to be exceeded until the plague was at its height in June 1646. One of these burials was of a soldier and two of 'strangers' but the large number of children (11) suggests that this was not typhus but some other form of viral infection. By December, with typhus raging throughout the town, the next four months were to witness 86 burials of which only 11 were children. This outbreak was further exacerbated by the second siege, which took place between 29 February and 21 March 1644. It is important to stress that these burial totals were not inflated by the deaths of soldiers or strangers. As figure 4.4 clearly shows they never accounted for more than 8 per cent of an annual total. Where ordinary soldiers were buried is unclear but they certainly do not appear in Newark's burial registers in any great numbers and those who do figure are predominantly officers.

Figure 4.4 Baptism and Burials, 1642-1648

Year	Burials	Percentage of soldier and stranger burials	Baptisms	Baptisms over burials
1642	87	-	98	+11
1643	194	3.1%	131	-63
1644	217	5.1%	155	-62
1645	160	7.5%	170	+10
1646	177	8.0%	85	-92
1647	48	-	64	+16
1648	52	-	94	+42
Totals	935	-	797	-138

Following the defeat of the king's Northern Army and Prince Rupert's Army at Marston Moor on the 2 July 1644, the garrison numbers at Newark were considerably increased by an influx of Royalist soldiers escaping southwards. By October, however, local Parliamentarians were gaining the upper hand and throughout the winter they began to tighten their grip around Newark. Though not besieged, the people of Newark were greatly restricted in their movements into the surrounding countryside at a time when there were considerable demands upon their store of provisions. Not until the arrival of Sir Marmaduke Langdale with 1,500 horse on 25 February 1645 was this situation reversed.[174] During this traumatic period, Newark experienced the worst of its typhus outbreaks with the period from November to April witnessing 108 burials of which only 11 were children. Although only six soldiers appear in the burial register (1 Major, 1 Lieutenant and 4 Captains) the epidemic does appear to have fallen quite severely upon the town's 'natural rulers'. It claimed the Mayor, Hercules Clay, an alderman, two of the town's knights and five gentlemen. Such a large number of fatalities amongst the town's social elite had not been known for decades and conditions within the garrison must have been truly dire to produce such a catastrophe. The impact of this epidemic upon ordinary troops within the garrison is not known since none appear in the registers; although it would seem extremely unlikely that their number was spared.

Typhus made its final wartime appearance in the town over the winter of 1645-1646. By then the king's cause was in terminal decline with his field armies defeated and local garrisons either surrendering on terms or falling to violent attacks.[175] Conditions within the town were particularly grim with the garrison being closely besieged from November 1645 through to its surrender in May 1646. For four consecutive months (December to March) the minimum number of burials per month was 20, a figure reached on only four occasions over the previous ten years. The full impact of this outbreak, however, was quickly overshadowed by the first signs of a more feared epidemic in the town, that of plague. The high figures for December and January were probably typhus related but from March onwards plague deaths began to fill the registers. We shall return to this epidemic later.

The winter months proved to be a period of high mortality for the citizens of Newark, exacerbated further by the fact that the three sieges experienced by the town occurred during this season. The summer months brought different diseases into the town with a variety of fevers, sicknesses and possibly dysentery. Over the period 1642-1646, four of the largest monthly mortality totals occurred during the summer months. Between May and August 1644, 80 burials were recorded of which 18 were children. The same period in 1643 witnessed 65 burials, but of these 34 (just under 53 per cent) were children. Whilst the evidence is far from conclusive, it does suggest that over the period of the war the winter months were less healthy for adults but that children were more at risk during the summer. In 1646, the town was visited by an epidemic that made little distinction between the ages, thrived during the summer months and was more lethal than typhus; the much feared plague. By the late summer of 1646 this epidemic had fanned out into the surrounding villages, decimating the local population. The significance of this plague epidemic is such that it needs to be examined independently from other contagious diseases.

The micro-organism Pasteurelle Pestis causes plague. It can manifest itself in three forms: bubonic, pneumonic and septicemic.[176] The form that appeared in Newark over this period was probably bubonic. The bacteria enter the body of a person when an infected flea, which has lost its usual rat host, bites them. The incubation period of bubonic plague is usually two to six days and it has a mortality rate of up to 60 per cent in certain circumstances. The rat that carried the plague flea was the black house rat *(Rattus rattus)*, which was a timid fragile creature, unlike its larger brown cousin, and lived in thatch roofs and clay walls of cottages. In the British climate, the black rat cannot survive for any length of time outside the warmth of a human dwelling and so plague is usually an urban disease; a pestilence of towns and cities that occasionally visited rural areas. Infection was usually introduced into a community by three methods. An infected person could carry the disease or flea with him; the fleas were brought into a town on infested merchandise, usually cloth; or the rats themselves were unwittingly carried on human transport. The disease often began in ports, introduced by fleas on infected ships from the continent, and it made its way up estuaries and navigable rivers on barges. Likewise the carrying of grain between counties in times of dearth or war may have led to the transportation of infected rodents.

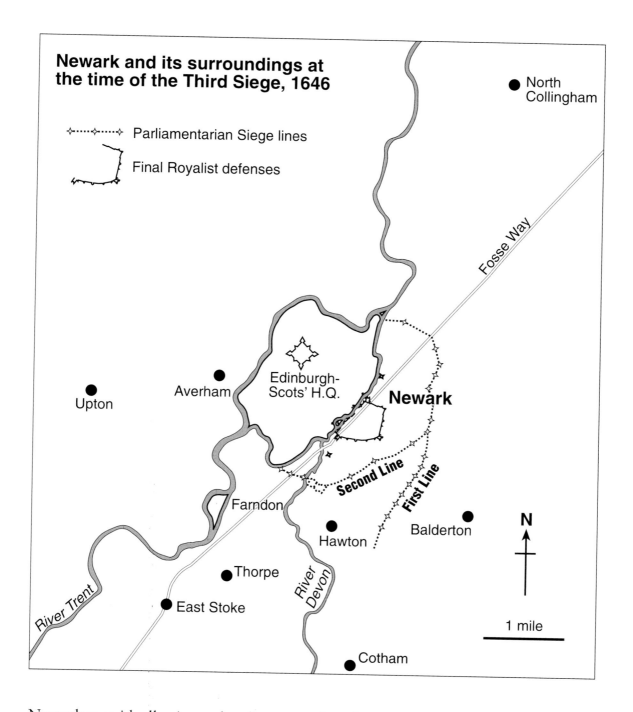

Newark and its surroundings at the time of the Third Siege, 1646

◇·····◇·····◇ Parliamentarian Siege lines

⌐¬ Final Royalist defenses

North Collingham

Fosse Way

Edinburgh-Scots' H.Q.

Averham

Upton

Newark

Second Line

First Line

Farndon

Hawton

Balderton

N

Thorpe

River Devon

River Trent

East Stoke

1 mile

Cotham

Newark was ideally situated to be exposed to the risk of plague, although the last major outbreak prior to 1645-46 had occurred over the years 1606-1607. Situated on the Great North Road by the river Trent and also a major market town for the area, large crowds of people travelled to or passed through the town. By the end of 1645 with its overcrowded streets, numerous visitors and stock piling of grain for a prolonged siege, it proved to be very receptive to the transmission of plague.[177]

Amongst the miscellaneous papers of the Borough Corporation are some accounts which clearly show that the plague commenced towards the end of 1645 and that a number of the expenses incurred were defrayed by the churchwardens.[178] A note on the back of one of these bills also states that the various sums spent on plague relief at this time came from the 'collection money on fast dayes' held at St. Mary Magdalene's. As early as 6 October 1645, the authorities paid out the sum of £1 'to the Doctors for searching ye corps at William Hayes'. There was already a growing concern that more than typhus might be lurking in the town. By the middle of November, plague was clearly identified within the community. An account submitted by the churchwarden Robert Gonison to the Corporation (himself later a victim to the plague) spells out the initial response to the outbreak'.

For ye visited hous by Mr Maiors commend in ye Town Novm 15	))	16s. 0d
For oatmeale to ye visited people Nov 15		14s. 6d
For coales to ye visited people Nov 15		7s. 6d
For oatmeale more to ye visited house Nov 19		4s. 8d
Paid to Richard Dykes and his partner for looking to ye visited people Novmbr 21	))	16s. 4d[179]

By December, as burials in the churchyard dramatically increased to over 20, further expenses were noted.

Paid more to Whittington for watching the sick folkes by Mr Maiors command Dec 13	))	8s
30 Dec 1645 Warrant to Pay Edward Hunt £3.6s.6d for beere to the visite house.		
4 Jan 1646 Delivered in salt and candles for the visited people at severall times	))	£1. 5s. 6d[180]

The above accounts appear to suggest that at this early stage an isolation hospital or 'pesthouse' was established in which infected people were quarantined. As the outbreak exploded in the spring and summer of 1646 it became necessary to quarantine whole families, both the sick and the well, in their own homes with watchers being paid to impose the confinement. During the early stage the authorities either believed they could control the outbreak or, more likely, the early infections were predominantly amongst soldiers at the garrison and could only be dealt with at a 'pesthouse'. If the latter is the case, this might explain why the burial registers do not initially identify this outbreak. In November there were only 6 burials recorded although by December this had risen to 21 of which just under half

(10) were children. This is a very different mortality pattern to that of typhus where very few children died. If the early victims of plague in 1645 were soldiers, this may possibly explain why the registers were devoid of detail. Throughout the autumn of 1645 (September through to December) only two soldiers appeared in the burial registers, a Captain Parsons and a Colonel Charles Leake. The daughter of a Captain Malbury was also buried. No ordinary soldiers are identified at all; as victims of plague with little financial means the churchyard may have been closed to them. Certainly their absence from the register (only 4 ordinary soldiers are listed for the whole of the war) suggests that those killed at the garrison were buried elsewhere.

Plague was probably brought into the town by Royalist troops joining the garrison during these closing months of the war. This, at least, was considered to be the cause by one contemporary observer within the town: John Twentyman writing of the year 1646 recorded 'the plague being brought in among them by soldiers which came from some other places'.[181] On 14 October 1645, King Charles arrived at the garrison with 800 horse, the remnants of his field army, and remained in the town for just under a month.[182] Much more significantly on 16 October, Prince Rupert and the remnants of his 300 horse arrived at Newark. Rupert had surrendered the town of Bristol to Parliament on 11 September. The king on hearing of the prince's action had him cashiered and suggested that he should seek his fortune overseas. Rupert had ridden to Newark to defend both his actions and honour before his uncle, the king. At the time when Rupert left Bristol plague was raging in the town to such an extent that the victorious Parliamentarians felt it wise to dispatch most of their army further a field until the pestilence had subsided.[183] The plague was probably carried to Newark therefore by Rupert's troops and by the time both he and the king had left in November it had become well established. Through January and February 1646 its symptoms remained dormant as a consequence of the severe winter cold.[184] Mortality rates were still high for these months (24 and 20 respectively) but the spread of victims was in keeping with another typhus epidemic.

The milder weather of March 1646 heralded a new outbreak of plague across the town, and on the 9 March, the mayor and aldermen issued public orders for its control. Their instructions were duly recorded in the Borough minute book and included the following:

> That the Justices of the Peace, Aldermen, and Coadjutors hereunder
> named, shall in their several divisions hereunder mentioned from time
> to time during this visitation take order that sufficient relief be provided,
> not only for such townsmen as are or shall be visited or infected, but
> also for all other poor persons, to prevent their wandering abroad.

> That they shall daily take a street account of all persons that shall be sick
> or die within their divisions, to the end that if upon search such persons
> shall be found to be infected, that then their house may be forthwith shut
> up, and a guard set upon the same, to prevent the further spread of such
> infection.

> ...It is ordered and agreed upon and directed that there shall be two
> searchers appointed and sworn to survey all persons sick or dying,
> and that they shall receive for their pains at the rate of 6d. per diem
> a piece, beside their further livelihood and subsistence.

> That the said Aldermen and Coadjutors shall within their divisions
> assign unto them appoint such a number of watchmen for the
> guarding of such houses as are or shall be infected as they shall think
> fit, and every such watchman for warding by day shall be allowed 8d.,
> and for warding by night 10d.

> That persons shall be nominated and appointed to bury all such
> persons as shall die of this infection.

> That such as shall die infected shall be buried in a place called
> Appleton about the midst thereof, and that special order shall be
> taken that their graves be made of sufficient depth.[185]

The survival of these plague orders is particularly helpful in allowing us to see how the pestilence was policed at its height, but they also raise some interesting questions. The opening paragraph makes it clear that these orders related to the townspeople and the monitoring of infection within their homes; there are no instructions regarding infection within the garrison quarters and what the Orders do not clarify is whether the control of plague amongst soldiers remained a purely military matter with which the civilian authorities were not encouraged to interfere. The everyday relationship between Governor and Corporation in the face of this epidemic is not spelt out, but a working compromise must have been arrived at. It is likely that in the midst of a siege, the harassed Governor transferred infected soldiers to the care of the Corporation and their 'pesthouse'.

The establishment of a plague burial plot or pit at Appleton is another area of special interest. The pit was clearly separated from the churchyard, but whether burials within it were entered in the register of St. Mary Magdalene Church is unclear; technically the register was a list of churchyard burials only. It is clear from surviving wills that where plague victims had specified and paid for internment in the churchyard (such as the baker Christopher Richards and alderman William Barrett) this occurred and was duly recorded.[186] A number of testators, however, who did die at Newark during the plague, do not appear in the burial registers. Amongst this group were Thomas Roughton and his wife, John Gill and Thomas Wogden. Roughton is particularly significant because in the Corporation minutes of May 1646 it is recorded

Thomas Roughton by his will in writeinge dated the tenth day of
Aprill 1646 gave to the towne of Newarke a Legacie of xx li in these
words 'xx li to the towne of Newarke to the best use the(y) can put it to' wch
was received by Mr Maior & imployed towards the maintenance of the
poore this year in the time of visitacion of the plague[187].

It appears that both Roughton and his wife 'died at this time', for his will specified that this was the only circumstance in which the money was to be handed over to the Corporation. There was clearly serious under-registration of deaths in the burial register but whether this relates only to those buried at Appleton we can only speculate. It is important to point out, however that the issue of under-registration appears to have preceded the outbreak of plague. The churchwarden's accounts record expenditures of money to purchase 'winding sheets and inkles' for the deceased poor of the town prior to plague. In a number of cases the deceased is identified; Widow Swinburn, Thomas Holland, Thomas Cheverall and also 'a poor drowned child' whose name was unknown.[188] None of these individuals are named in the burial register and if this was the case prior to the plague, it is not amiss to assume even more omissions in the face of an epidemic.

Another undated receipt in the borough's miscellaneous papers that clearly relates to the 1645/46 epidemic may well originate from early on in the outbreak. Its contents reflect another aspect of the battle against the pestilence. The bill records the following;

An Ante dote	6s. 8d
Harthorne & Marygold flowers	2s. 0d.
The Ante dote	6s. 8d
The same Agayne	6s. 8d

Frankinscence	1s. 0d
A fumeing powder	4s. 6d
A Cataplasme	3s. 6d
Mithridate & syrup of maydenhare	1s. 0d
A perfumeing powder	4s. 6d[189]

The quantities involved suggest that the above supplies would not have been adequate for the whole town and raises the possibility that they were for use either at the pesthouse or for Corporation members and their families. The materials listed reflect contemporary views on the transmission of the disease and its treatment. Plague was believed to be spread by miasma, 'stinking vapours by which the air is putrefied'[190] 'Unburied corpses and stagnant pools, along with the stink of graveyards' were thought to be the real cause of plague. This explains the Corporation's order that care was to be taken to ensure that corpses were buried at the appropriate depth at Appleton.

The burning of incense and perfume and the use of sweet smelling powders to scent the air were believed to counter the effects of miasma. The most popular medicines for victims of plague were theriac, commonly called 'treacle', and mithridatium. During this period, all who could afford them used drinks and potions compounded of rue, rosemary, onions, wormwood, mithridatium and treacle. The antidote identified in this bill was probably made of some, if not all of these ingredients. Although Newark was experiencing increasing shortages because of the siege, it does appear that medical supplies, albeit in small quantities, were still being brought into the town.

A bill dating from early 1646 identified those parts of the town were plague was most severe during the opening months.

A Bill for bread for the vizitted for barnebee gate and norgate and the tonne to me Samuell Cole	))	£4.16s.6d[191]

Both Barnby Gate and North Gate were areas adjacent to the outer defences constructed just before the start of the third siege. Because a considerable amount of housing had been demolished during construction of ramparts and ditches, the two districts were greatly overcrowded. Barnby Gate and North Gate were also two of the poorest areas of Newark in the seventeenth century, both having a large numbers of poor quality houses. In the 1664 hearth tax returns of the 45 households identified in Barnby Gate, 42 only had one hearth and of these 33 (just over 73 per cent) were exempt from payment owing to poverty. In North Gate 42 of the 55 households had only one hearth and 29 of these (just under 53 per cent) were exempt. Poverty and overcrowding made these two areas particularly susceptible to disease. Surprisingly they were quite a distance from the corn market and mill area, where rats were likely to have been most numerous, but main streets ran through both districts and they were situated next to town gates. By this stage, plague victims and their families were being quarantined in their own homes and in order to stop them wandering abroad, bread was being delivered. A further expenditure of £2.2s was recorded on the bill for ale being taken to these households. A concerted effort was being made in the town to limit the spread of the infection, but to little avail.

Whilst plague was raging in the garrison of Newark during April and May, the besieging Parliamentarian army under General Poyntz appears to have been unaffected by the epidemic. Within the numerous pieces of correspondence between the military authorities and Parliament there is no mention of any infection within the army and the parish registers of villages such as Farndon and Balderton are devoid of plague deaths. In a letter dated 3 March 1646, the Earl of Rutland wrote that 'the soldiers were all full of courage, and very few sick amongst them'.[192] The presence of around 16,000 troops created considerable economic problems for these communities, as witnessed by the numerous petitions they sent to the 'Committee of Lords and Commons' but the close confinement of Newark limited the spread of infection.[193]

The Newark garrison surrendered on 6 May 1646 and two days later between 1500 and 1800 soldiers marched out of the town. This was a day earlier than originally agreed owing precisely to the presence of plague in the town. A contemporary witness noted of Newark;

> And truely it is become a miserable stinking infected towne. I pray
> God they do not infect the counties and townes adjacent, which is the
> care of the commissioners to prevent[194]

The witness's anxiety about the infection being dispersed across the county once the siege was lifted was now about to be fulfilled. At the start of the siege in November 1645, after the governor had sent 1,000 of his horse to Lichfield, one account claimed that the remaining garrison consisted of 800 horse and 3000 infantry and with the aid of 1,000 townsmen.[195]   Whilst these figures were probably an exaggeration, they do suggest that the garrison was considerably larger at the start of the siege than at its ending.   A combination of military action, and more significantly plague infection, had devastated the army of Newark.

With the ending of the war, Newark became demilitarised, but plague continued to ravage the town.   Lucy Hutchinson noted after the surrender that the pestilence 'was so raging there that it almost desolated the place'.[196]   In June, the burial register recorded the internment of 32 individuals in the churchyard, the largest monthly total on record for the century.   July faired little better with 27 burials noted.   Burials at Appleton were probably not part of these totals for Newark and so the final figure was likely to be considerably more than this.   Groups of people from Newark were also roaming or lodging in the surrounding countryside in an attempt to avoid the pestilence.   The constable's account's for Upton, which lay just over 5 miles away from Newark, recorded in 1646;

> Payd the 26th of May for Bread, Cheese & Beere for six people of
> Newark which the watchmen kept out of the town the(y) desiringe releife,
> returned to the wood.[197]

Behind these figures lay many family tragedies.   Robert Gonison (or Gomston), the churchwarden at Newark whose bills at the end of 1645 testified to the arrival of plague in the town, found his own family infected in June 1646.   Within 21 days he and four of his children were dead.   Such was the suddenness with which death struck the family that a nuncupative will had to be made by Gonison and registered by his wife in 1647.[198]   In the same month the Knight household contracted the plague and within 6 days William, his wife Ellen, and their two children were all dead.   Similar stories could be told in many parts of the town.

The seriousness of the epidemic is further hinted at in two wills from the period. alderman William Barrett and baker Christopher Richards both died in July 1646, most likely from plague.   In their wills they were moved to bequeath the sums of £40 and £3 respectively to assist the 'poore visited people of Newarke'.   With little opportunity for trade or travel, charity was essential for many ordinary citizens just to obtain food. The ordinary routines of trade, commerce and travel were severely curtailed by the epidemic, and not until 1647 would things begin to regain some form of normality.   Two of the town's aldermen, John Queningborough and William

Baker, had been identified by the victorious Parliamentarians as Royalist delinquents, but were unable to compound for their estates within the specified period after the surrender.[199] Other inhabitants were also unable to compound because of the plague. Thomas Hobman an ironmonger from Newark petitioned the Committee for Compounding in May 1647 that 'he may be admitted to compound for his delinquency as if he had come in according to the time limited'.[200] The presence of plague made it impossible for them to travel outside the area.

Within six weeks of the surrender of Newark, the plague began to decimate the town's satellite villages. It was probably carried into these communities by fleeing inhabitants and the return of local conscripted labourers who had dismantled the garrison's defences. Throughout the months July to September, the epidemic was rampant in the parish of Farndon, two miles away from Newark. Over the period 1643-45, the average number of burials per year in Farndon was 14, whilst 1647-48 only averaged 6 per annum. In 1646 there were 62 of which 32 (just under 52 per cent) were in July and August. This was a crisis mortality ratio of 4.4, the highest for a century. An entry in the register possibly suggests how the infection was brought into the village.

> William Jackson, a souldier was buryed July 29th 1646.[201]

In the parish of Balderton, again only two miles away Newark, there had been 19 burials in 1645. In 1646, 'the yeare of the plague', this had risen to 129 giving a crisis mortality rate of around 6.8. In North Collingham (six miles from Newark) the parish register records the burial of 32 persons who died of plague over the period 11 August to 23 December 1646 when a comment in the margin duly notes that the 'plague ceased'. The burial registers of Averham, Cotham, Hawton, Kelham and Thorpe, all within a radius of four miles of Newark, either have gaps in their registers for the period or are now missing. There can be little reason to doubt, however, that they too were decimated by plague. Farms would have been left empty and the economic and commercial life of communities shattered, as well as the unquantifiable emotional costs to their citizens.

The registers of East Stoke (just under four miles from Newark) give further evidence of how the infection fanned out from Newark to its satellite villages. Newark castle and its adjacent meadows were actually part of East Stoke parish at this time, which makes its experience of greater significance.[202] In 1645 there had been 9 burials and the annual average for the previous decade had been 7. In 1646, the parish was devastated by plague with 169 burials being recorded. Of these entries, 159 had been marked with a cross clearly identifying them as plague victims. The register noted

> All those names that have ye crosse before them did dye of ye plague;
> From which plague good Lord deliver us[203]

This was a crisis mortality rate of 24.1; a figure hardly surpassed even in the worst of the plague outbreaks in London during the seventeenth century. The first plague death was recorded on 28 May but it was not until the end of July that it really took hold. Amongst some of its earliest victims were 'Thomas Pattisson formerly a souldier died of the plague and was buried in the fields the 28th July' and 'Peeter and John Haselam that came from Newark and borded at William Symsons'. Newark residents were recorded amongst the victims again in August when 'Francis Moate of Newarke' and his wife are named in the burial register. In September 'Leeftenant Wright that lodged at Hugh Baguleys' (brother of the parish clerk) and a 'youth from Newarke that lodged at Hugh Baguleys' as well as Mary Green 'the daughter in law of Francis Moate' all died of plague. During the same month two maids and a servant also died of the plague and their surnames suggest that they came from the Newark area. Once the infection had been carried into a house, it was not uncommon for the whole household to become infected. The Baguleys, Symsons and Pattison families were virtually wiped out by the epidemic. In early September the parish clerk Robert Baguley caught the plague and made his final will on 7 September 1646. Having recorded so many deaths in the register he now sensed that his own name would be added, but by another hand. He commented of the situation that these were

> dangerous times of God of heavie judgements of the plauge and
> pestilence amongst us.[204]

These tantalising remnants of local registers all suggest that a number of townspeople from Newark died in the surrounding parishes. The total numbers that succumbed to the disease were far in excess of the 200 names that appear in St. Mary Magdalene's parish registers over the period 1645-46.

By the end of July 1646, the desperate plight of the various plague-infected communities encouraged the newly established authorities into a vigorous effort to fund relief by both assessment and brief. The constable's accounts at Upton recorded that they spent 1s.6d when they met

> With the chiefe constable & Mr Baker the 19th of August
> comminge for assessments both for Nottingham & for
> visited towns.[205]

On the 10 September, they handed over a payment of £1.6s.8d for the relief of 'visitted townes' and a second payment of 6s.8d was made on the 8 October. By the time of the second payment, the rate of infection was on the decline but the needs of the survivors were as great as ever. Similarly, the account book of the parish of Thorpe-by-Newark noted a 'levie for the relief of Balderton plague victims', which amounted to a weekly rate of 5s.6d for two months.[206] Across the whole of the county monies were raised and in a number of surviving church account books there are references to sums raised by communities who themselves were still recovering from the consequences of the war.

The years 1642-1646 were truly a time of death and disease not only for soldiers but also for the citizens of Newark. Despite under-registration and the failure to record soldiers' burials accurately, if at all, the registers do display the general demographic trend experienced by the town (see particularly Figure 4.4). These five years witnessed 835 burials but only 639 baptisms, giving a surplus of 196 recorded burials. To this figure needs to be added those individuals who failed to be entered in the registers, either through oversight or because they were not actually buried in the churchyard. Behind this simple arithmetic lies the stark reality that three of these five years (1643, 1644 and 1646) all witnessed crisis mortality ratios ranging from just under 2.0 up to 2.4 of the 1636-1640 mean (90.2 burials per year).

The amounts received by the churchwardens in burial fees supports these mortality trends. In 1641 and 1642, fees amounting to £12.2s.11d and £11.5s.2d respectively were received. By 1643, the total had risen to £22.16s and the largest sum for the war occurred in 1644 when £33.7s.9d was paid. During the year of the plague, burial fees for the churchyard amounted to £29.5s.11d. The churchwarden accounts began on Lady Day (March 25) and ended on March 24 the year following; thus the accounts for 1644 ran through to March 1645. Because entries are not adequately dated, expenditure cannot be allocated to each Gregorian calendar year (beginning January 1). Even so, they do bear out the broad demographic trends identified in the other sources. The year 1643 proved to be a severe one for infant mortality with 79 children's burials recorded; a crisis mortality ratio of nearly 2.5 that of the 1636-1640 mean of 32.4. The majority of these burial entries over this period were for Newark citizens, not soldiers or strangers, and so the short-term effect on the town's population would have been substantial. Although plague claimed a large number of lives over the period 1645-46, by far the biggest killer of ordinary citizens was typhus. It occurred with lethal regularity over the winter months and may account for up to 30 per cent of those whose names appear in the burial registers.

The question of soldier burials in towns besieged during the Civil War has not been adequately answered, and the example of Newark highlights the problems which parish registers often pose. Throughout the war, the names of 28 officers and 4 solders only are entered in the burial register. The names of soldiers also fail to appear in any great number in the registers of adjacent parishes. In a garrison the size of Newark, with all the military action it witnessed as well as epidemics, it is highly unlikely that so few perished. Other evidence such as newsbooks and military memoirs support this assertion. During the siege of York, numerous burials of soldiers are recorded in the registers of that town's parish churches, but at Newark there remains no record of where its soldiers were buried.[207] They may have been buried *en masse* in the churchyard with no effort being made to record their details, or they may have been buried elsewhere. An examination of Newark's churchwarden accounts, alongside those entries contained in the parish registers, suggest that the former, rather than the latter, may have been the case for the early part of the war at least. At the end of the 1643 accounts there are two entries recording the purchase of a 'winding sheet and inkle for prince Rupert's soldiers' at 2s a time. In 1644, 3s.4d was spent on burying a further two soldiers and on August 15 2s more was spent on burying another soldier from the garrison. These five soldiers were all buried in the churchyard but they do not appear in the burial register. We know about them because they were provided with winding sheets at the expense of the parish, others may not have been so fortunate. In 1645, Richard Yoxall and Ralph Walker were paid 3s.4d for 'passing bells and macking soldiers graves by Mr Maiors command'. This was an extra payment for additional duties and the amount paid suggests that this was a mass burial not a single internment. The usual fee for a burial ranged from 3d up to 1s, depending upon the place and type of grave. A few weeks later they were paid a further 3s.6d 'for grave making by Mr Maiors command'. The burial register makes no mention of this additional work and no soldiers are identified in them at this time. As the war progressed, a separate burial plot for garrison soldiers may have been established. By the time of the plague, it is not unlikely that soldier's corpses were deposited at Appleton with little thought about recording their details. Many a mother or wife would never discover where their loved ones were buried.

These periods of heavy mortality would have been marked by constant activity amongst the burial plots, and the doleful – almost continuous – tolling of the church bells. Indeed the level of use meant that the bells came to require additional maintenance. In 1644 (217 burials) and 1646 (177 burials) annual sums of £4.15s.5d, and £4.4s.1d was paid out on them. By contrast, in 1645 (160 burials) the parish only needed to spend £2.18s.8d on the bells. The spire and bells at St. Mary Magdalene were the pride of the town and their maintenance was always high on the parish agenda. Extensive burials in the churchyard meant additional payments for its up keep, even after Appleton was opened. In 1644 Richard Smith was paid 5s 'for leading manure out of the churchyard'. Between October and November 1645, 'when ye king was in towne' the warden's accounts record the expenditure of £1.8s on dressing and cleaning the churchyard. On 27 August 1647 they had to spend a further 12s on the yard. Regular sums of this magnitude had not been lavished on the churchyard during the whole of the preceding century. Probably the most telling entry is that for 6 March 1647 when a new spade and shovel were purchased for 2s.8d; the old ones having probably been worn out by constant use over the past 18 months. Such was the turmoil of this plague period that the churchwardens were not able to finalise their accounts for 1646 until the end of May 1647, and by then the war had ended. From January 1647, burials diminished considerably with only 100 individuals recorded in the register over the next 24 months; less than half that of the 1644 total. Over this same period baptisms began to increase and for the first time in many years there was a surplus of births over burials for two consecutive years, which amounted to 158.

Although failing to provide a comprehensive picture of all deaths in Newark, the town's registers do clearly show that both typhus and plague cut a swathe through a large portion of the civil population. During the five-year period of conflict, 835 burials were recorded of which only 29 per cent were children. The majority of deaths were of local adults with only 43 individuals being identified as 'strangers' or soldiers. The severity of this mortality crisis can be clearly ascertained when compared to the burial figures for the previous two decades (1621-30 and 1631-40) when burials for both periods totalled 896. The three typhus epidemics between 1643 and 1646 probably killed between 12 and 15 per cent of the town's population as well as numerous soldiers who failed to appear in the burial registers. The demographic consequences of the plague (which occurred over 1645-46) are more difficult to quantify because of under-registration and deaths that occurred outside the town. A petition to the Committee for Compounding from the inhabitants of Newark dated 21 January 1647 pleaded for further time to pay their fines because 'the plague has consumed over 1000 persons and the town is not yet clear'.[208] Even though this figure may be an exaggeration (it possibly includes numbers from surrounding parishes) it still reflects the seriousness with which the epidemic was viewed within the town. From burial entries in the town's registers and those of the surrounding parishes, as well as details contained in wills, it would appear, that not less than 300 inhabitants from Newark perished in the epidemic; around 15 per cent of the population. Together, therefore, typhus and plague may have killed between 25 and 30 per cent of the town's population over the period of the first Civil War. These percentages are comparable to those identified for Civil War Bristol by Paul Slack, although the numbers are much less because Bristol had a population of around 11,000 compared with Newark's 2,000.[209] Unlike Bristol, however, the potential for a quick recovery for Newark was more limited. With few of the economic opportunities that a large mercantile city presented, population recovery was always going to be a drawn out affair. Even allowing for under-registration of houses, hearth tax returns of 1674 suggest that the town's population had still not recovered to its 1640 level. The consequences of disease associated with Civil War conditions, therefore, had a longer effect upon the town than the fighting itself.

PLATE 1. Newark Castle; the west curtain wall. The castle owes its present semi-ruinous state to an order issued by the victorious Parliamentarians that it be demolished by the townsfolk of Newark. Owing to the poor conditions (plague and malnutrition) that prevailed in the town after the surrender, however, the work was never completed.

PLATE 2. Newark Castle; gatehouse and north-west tower.

PLATE 3.
Newark Castle;
12th century
gatehouse.

PLATE 4. Newark Castle; Middle Tower in the west curtain wall.

PLATE 5.
The parish church
of St.Mary
Magdalene,
Newark-on-Trent.

PLATE 6.
The spire of the
parish church of
St.Mary Magdalene
from which John
Twentyman
witnessed Prince
Rupert lift the
Second Siege of
Newark as he
defeated the
Parliamentarian
forces ranged
around the town.

PLATE 7. Newark Market Place; the Olde White Hart Inn. The inn was headquarters for Colonel William Staunton's regiment.

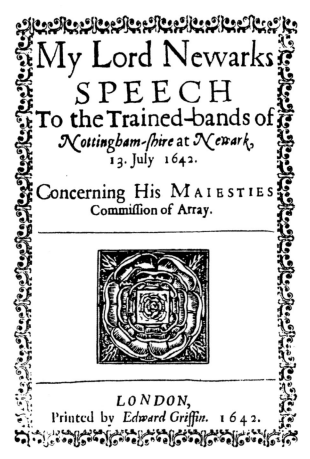

My Lord Newarks
SPEECH
To the Trained-bands of
Nottingham-shire at Newark,
13. July 1642.

Concerning His MAIESTIES
Commiffion of Array.

LONDON,
Printed by Edward Griffin. 1642.

PLATE 8. Pamphlet recording the speech delivered to the Trained Bands of Nottingham at Newark assembled at the instruction of Charles I who was present in the town.

PLATE 9.
Prince Rupert who
lifted the Second
Siege of Newark in
1644 but finally
resigned from
service to his uncle,
Charles I, following
the latter's criticism
of Rupert's decision
to surrender the
town of Bristol.

PLATE 10. The
Governor's House,
Stodman Street,
Newark. As its
name suggests, it
was here that
Newark's Civil War
governors are said
to have been based
at the time of the
three sieges. It was
here too that the
king, Charles I, is
said to have
quarrelled with his
nephew, Prince
Rupert, over the
surrender of Bristol
in September 1645.

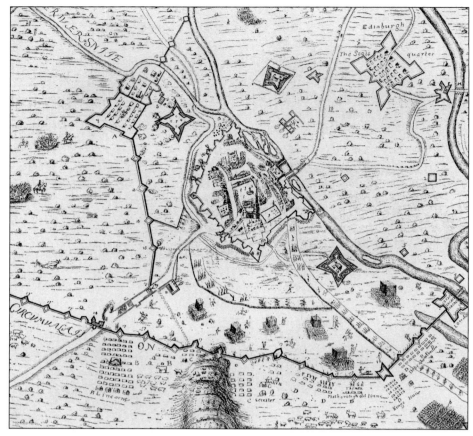

PLATE 11. Detail from a Parliamentarian plan of the Third Siege of Newark, 1645-1646, drawn by Richard Clampe. The map is oriented with West at the top and shows the town of Newark defended by a ditch and rampart, punctuated with regular bastions for cannon.

The two outlying Royalist forts – the King's Sconce and the Queen's Sconce – are shown alongside the river either side of the town. The large fort of the Scottish army – called 'Edinburgh' – is at the top right of the picture.

The 'circumvalation' or line of Parliamentary ramparts stretches along the foot of the illustration, behind which various named regiments are encamped on either side of Beacon Hill (bottom, centre). Nearby are 'squares' of foot soldiers with pikemen surrounded by musketeers, and over to the left of the picture are regiments of mounted cavalry.

On the slopes of Beacon Hill sheep and cattle are shown quietly grazing, tended by a shepherd who appears to be asleep! Clampe was anxious to point out that the owners of the livestock 'never receved during the siedge any loss or damage in any of them in the least'.

[Notes by Sharon Ingham].

PLATE 12. Newark siege coin minted during the time of the third and final siege. Such coins were made of silver plate and struck for values ranging from 6d. to 2s.6d. The abbreviation 'OBS' comes from the Latin 'obsessum' meaning 'besieged'.

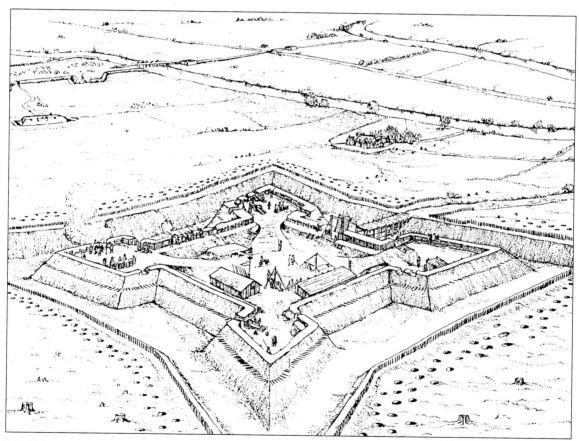

PLATE 13. An artist's impression of the Queen's Sconce at Newark. The Queen's Sconce – together with its northern counterpart, the King's Sconce (now demolished) – was built by the Royalists to protect the town from attack. It survives to this day and is considered one of the best surviving Civil War earthworks anywhere in the country. Gillian Elias' drawing suggests how the Queen's Sconce might have appeared when garrisoned at the time of the Third Siege.

PLATES 14-16. A selection of Civil War artefacts found around Newark. Above, spilling from the brown glazed jug in which they were found, and arranged upon a contemporary Civil war pamphlet, is a selection of lozenge-shaped Newark siege coins unearthed at Crankley Point to the north of the town. Also from the Crankley Point Civil War Hoard are a 17th century thimble and sealing wax case. Three Charles I gold coins (dated 1626 – 1627) are also included in the picture as are three lead musket balls and a selection of differently sized Civil War canon balls, all found in the Newark area. The light coloured canon ball is made of stone.

Right and below is a sword with shark skin handle and hand guard, also found in the Newark area. The blade bears the name of the renowned swordmaker Andrea Ferara.

CHAPTER 5

'What is the city but the people?':
Marriage, childbirth, commerce and community in a time of war and disruption

Whilst the consequences of war can never be over-estimated, the resilience and ability of both individuals and communities to maintain a state of normality and continuity often is. Both Corporation and ecclesiastical records from the period clearly demonstrate that Newark sought to run its communal activities as if the war and the subsequent Republic were not happening. Markets continued to be held, officials elected, and the poor and needy relieved. In spite of new civil legislation the church registers show that weddings continued and children were brought to be baptised. The period of the Civil Wars in England was one of both continuity and change and this chapter seeks to explore how both these realities were experienced.

According to the marriage service of the *Book of Common Prayer*, wedlock existed for the procreation of children, as a remedy against sinful desires, and for the creation of a mutual partnership of help and comfort. According to Cressy, over 80 per cent of all adults in seventeenth century England were married at some stage.[210] Demographic studies have shown that men were usually between 27 and 28 years of age at their first marriage, but that this could be affected by economic and social fluctuations. Because of high adult mortality it was not uncommon for individuals to experience several marriages as spouses died. These wider demographic trends were reflected in Newark with the turmoil and unrest of the 1640s having considerable implications for marriage patterns. A full reconstruction of Newark families lies beyond the scope of this work, so a detailed analysis of age, social background and family alliances is not possible. A basic analysis of statistical data extrapolated from the registers, however, can give an insight into trends and the significance of political events upon marriage in the town.

Over the decade 1630-1639 the pattern of weddings recorded in St. Mary's registers show a considerable degree of continuity and stability. The average annual rate for the decade is 18.7 (see Table 5.1) and apart from 1639 there appears to have been little fluctuation from this figure. Why 1639 should have witnessed such a rise in the number of weddings (28) is unclear. It might possibly be linked to the effects of the Bishop's Wars, which may have encouraged some couples to break the convention of delaying their marriage for several years. Throughout the decade, Lent was scrupulously observed with only two marriages occurring in March, and these managed to avoid the festival because Easter occurred later in those particular years. In 9 of the 10 years, 65 per cent or more of the marriages occurred between April and June and September to November. The Church of England maintained from its Catholic past a religious calendar prohibiting marriage during particular seasons of the liturgical year. These included the period of Lent mentioned above, Rogationtide and Trinity and the weeks of Advent before Christmas.[211] The distribution of marriages across the year in Newark reflects the liturgical cycle of prohibitions and as such probably differed little from that of other parishes across the country.

The decade that encompassed the Civil Wars in England (1639-1653) witnessed an increase in the number of marriages from 187 to 214, a rise of just under 15 per cent. This increase is particularly focussed on the years 1644-1646 when just fewer than 46 per cent of the decade's weddings (98) took place. Far from discouraging marriage, the uncertainty of the conflict appears to have removed many of the constraints upon early wedlock. The registers show that nearly all of these additional weddings were of local inhabitants, though it is possible that some of the men were serving as soldiers in the garrison. What is clear is that, according to the registers, these were not 'stranger weddings' or the consequence of outsiders moving into the town.

Prior to the outbreak of the Civil War the year 1641 witnessed 30 marriages - a figure that greatly exceeded the decennial average of 21.4. It is likely that the uncertainty of the times encouraged a number of Newark residents into earlier than planned nuptial arrangements. During the first two years of the war the number of weddings at Newark was reduced considerably with only 13 in 1642 and 11 (just over half the decennial average) in 1643. The year of the plague (1646) was a time that witnessed the greatest number of weddings over the decade. During the months March to July when the plague was at its fiercest there were no weddings recorded in the Newark registers. Just over 70 per cent (29) of the year's weddings occurred in the period August to November and six of those involved widows. Over the same period there were five weddings of Newark couples at the neighbouring parish of Farndon and four at Syerston. As with burials, there was considerable demographic activity both within and beyond the parish boundaries by the citizens of Newark. Once the epidemic had ended, the consolidation of family units and estates within the town went on at quite a pace.

The last three years of the 1640s were a time of considerable dearth in Newark, with many of the town's poor experiencing near starvation. This was not the time to either get married or raise a family, and this is reflected in the fact that in each of these years the number of weddings was considerably less than the decennial average. The year 1647 was particularly lean with only nine weddings recorded for the whole year. Although 1648 saw some improvement, the figure was still less than the previous decade's annual average.

The 1653 Marriage Act was to have a considerable impact upon the details recorded in the parish registers. This legislation instituted civil marriage before a Justice of the Peace or a prominent citizen of the town and made weddings performed solely by a clergyman in a church illegal. Marriages were henceforth to be recorded in a separate register kept by a Registrar. This civil ceremony was so unpopular that many couples often had both a civilian and a church wedding. In Newark the name of the Registrar, usually the Mayor is added to the church registers suggesting that this may have been the common practice for many of the town's citizens. Even so, there are no weddings recorded for the whole of 1653 and none in the first quarter of 1654, making a detailed assessment for this decade impossible for the historian. By the end of the 1650s annual marriage rates were returning to their mid 1630s level and a degree of normality appeared to be returning to the nuptial arrangements of Newark's citizens. What is significant, however, is that the seasons of prohibition continued to be observed by many couples throughout the 1650s - and this at a time when the Prayer Book was banned and the Anglican Church proscribed. Evidence from the registers suggests there was a degree of Anglican survivalism at a popular level within the parish (see Chapter 7).

The marriage details extrapolated from the registers of Newark testify to two diverse facts. Economic and political trends did have an effect upon marriage rates but they could never totally eliminate the basic human imperative to create stable family units and propagate society. In spite of war, pestilence and famine, couples continued to fall in love and create new families.

Table 5.1: Marriages at Newark 1631-1660[212]

Year	Number of marriages	Year	Number of marriages	Year	Number of marriages
1630	17	1640	23	1650	1*
1631	23	1641	30	1651	3*
1632	21	1642	13	1652	7
1633	23	1643	11	1653	0*
1634	20	1644	36	1654	19
1635	16	1645	21	1655	13
1636	10	1646	41	1656	20
1637	16	1647	9	1657	24
1638	13	1648	17	1658	21
1639	28	1649	13	1659	10
Decennial average	18.7		21.4		11.9

* = Incomplete or no entries for the year

The details relating to childbirth contained within the baptismal registers of the parish church testify to a general continuity of birth rates, but the years 1643-1645 witnessed a period of considerable upheaval. Between 1640 and 1645 the number of baptisms per annum doubled, mainly as a result of the influx of civilians during the period of fighting. Between 1640-1642 and 1646-1649 the average number of baptisms per annum was around 81, but the years 1643-1645 yielded figures of 131, 156 and 170 respectively.[213] None of these baptisms were identified as either strangers or travellers suggesting that the families were actually resident in the town at the time, paying their parish and church levies and meeting their military contributions. This increase in rates suggests that Newark had become a safe haven for families with Royalist sympathies from places as far away as Lincoln and Grantham as well as from adjacent parishes. This is further confirmed by the compounding records from the end of the war where a number of gentry in Lincolnshire are identified as having been at Newark in the service of the king.

Affluent enough to be able to leave their own homes, they would obviously have been in a position to pay the parish dues at their temporary homes in Newark.

The distribution of baptisms/births over the period 1643-1645 breaks the link with the seasonal and agricultural cycles identified both before and after the war.[214] Usually the months July-August were a period when the least number of baptisms were recorded, suggesting that conception rates were low from October to December. During the central period of the Civil War, however, the monthly distribution of baptisms remained relatively constant throughout the year. This may suggest that the strong links with agriculture, which had persisted in peacetime, were disrupted once the fighting began. Newark probably became a centre for drawing in the produce of surrounding villages, and less involved in the agricultural round of production. Indeed, many of the town's surrounding fields were taken over during the war to allow construction of the town defences. The number of births per annum was not severely reduced until the end of the 1640s and the early years of the 1650s when disease and poor harvest had reduced both the number and fertility of young couples. Children continued to be born and nurtured throughout the war, with new arrivals to the town doubling the birth rate during the fighting. Not until after the war had ended did figures return to their pre-war rate. Against this trend in births, however, must be set the huge increase in mortality identified earlier in chapter 4.

The widowed, orphaned, sick and poor were always vulnerable in seventeenth century England, but war and civil disturbance made their situation even more precarious. In the face of military assessments, free quarter and the collateral damage of warfare, the collection and distribution of poor rates often became difficult. Accounts from the Overseers of the Poor are rare survivals for seventeenth century Newark but the fortunate preservation of two sets of loose accounts, one for the year 1639-40 and the other for 1645-46, provide us with a useful insight into their application. More importantly they clearly demonstrate that a real attempt was made to continue the provision of relief for the 'impotent poor' even at the height of the war. The earlier accounts provide us with a peacetime baseline from which to assess the later figures (see Table 5.2).

Income over the year 1639-40 amounted to £51.18s.1d of which the Book of Assessment raised £48.19s, fines for moral misbehaviour amounted to 4s.4d and the remainder was carried forward from the previous year.[215] A sum of £3.8s remained uncollected at the end of the year. Throughout the year poor relief was distributed weekly, with the highest weekly payout amounting in total to 19s.4d, and the lowest 17s. The period 19 May to 30 June 1639 witnessed a succession of weeks where payouts were 19s or above; thereafter the amounts paid out were reduced considerably. This may suggest a period of sickness, perhaps a summer fever, which necessitated additional relief. At the end of the year the Overseers' account was in credit to the sum of £1.10s.1d.

Alongside this set of accounts there was also a list of recipients of Poor Relief over the year headed 'The Collectors Notes of Poor Persons'.[216] On this, 52 individuals are identified of which 22 (just fewer than 45 per cent) were widows. Weekly amounts paid out to the identified individuals varied from 2d to 1s (just two persons) and the amount they received was probably dependent upon personal circumstances.

Table 5.2: Poor Relief Details 1639-40 and 1645-46

Details	1639/40	1645/46
Book of Assessment	£48.19s.0d	£45.12s.8d
Fines received	4s.4d	
Persons not assessed		3s.4d
Moneys not received	£3.8s.0d	£7.10s.3d
Total Income	£51.18s.1d	£45.16s.0d
End of year Balance	+ £1.10s.1d	-£2.10s.4d
Heaviest period of payments	21 Apr – 30 June	Nov 23 - 1 March
Weekly Payments High	19s.4d	16s.10d
Low	17s	15s.3d

In 1645-46 the total amount collected by the Overseers was £45.18s, of which £45.12s 8d was from the assessment and a further 3s.4d came from non-assessed persons.[217] By the end of the year (24 March 1646) there still remained £7.10s.3d uncollected. The Assessment yielded less than that collected in peacetime and the amount uncollected was double that of the 1639-40 period; finances were apparently very stretched. The amount of need within the town was probably greater in 1645 than it had been for many decades, and the number of widows may well have been higher. The resources for providing relief, however, were considerably less. This is reflected in the weekly sums disbursed, the highest being 16s.10d (less than the lowest sum of 1639) and the lowest 15s.3d. Such lower payments probably enabled the resources to be spread more thinly. By the end of the year, however, the account was still in deficit to the tune of £2.10s.4d. The period of heaviest demand on the Poor Fund was from 23 November 1645 to 1 March 1646, which coincided with the start of the third and final siege. This was a period that witnessed both typhus and plague and at this early stage the additional financial measures needed to meet the outbreak of pestilence were not in place.

At a time of considerable financial and social upheaval, Newark's civic and religious authorities appear to have made considerable efforts to ensure the continuation of poor relief for the community's sick and vulnerable citizens. Although the Book of Assessment yielded decreasing sums and the accounts showed increasing deficits, a sense of religious and civic duty was not entirely undermined by the upheavals of war.

At the start of the Civil War, Newark was a centre for local commerce and trade. A market was held every Wednesday, which specialised in the buying and selling of cattle. Four great quarterly fairs or markets were also held and the Corporation organised an annual horse race on Coddington Moor on 4 May. With the outbreak of hostilities in 1642 this pattern was completely disrupted and the commercial life of the town was completely restructured. First to go appears to have been the Coddington races as many of the county's horses were commandeered for military service. Owners who had managed to protect their horses were loath to expose their animals to public (and more specifically military) scrutiny at such an event. The quarterly fairs fail to appear in the surviving records from 1643, and it is most likely that they too ceased to be held. By contrast, the weekly market does appear to have continued throughout the war and we note that John Martin, a butcher from Newark, was fined at the end of the war by parliament for his willingness to service the Royalist garrison with cattle and beef, irrespective of whether the meat had been plundered or legitimately brought to market.[218] Travel into and out of

Newark appears to have been largely unrestricted apart from those times when the town was actually under siege. The accounts of the constables for the nearby village of Upton frequently record 'for our charges when wee went to Newarke'. They also document a continuous flow of hay, corn, straw and livestock into the town. Again, an entry in the accounts at Upton noted

My charges when I went to newarke with corne
and we lay at Red Lodge all night.   4d.[219]

A large percentage of this agricultural produce went to the garrison as part of the community's military assessment but some of it would have ended up for sale in the town market to feed the civilian population. The presence of soldiers and the large numbers of Royalist families who had moved into the town for safety meant that there was always a heavy demand for food. This led to some shortages and a general increase in prices. The poor of Newark would have been particularly vulnerable to this war induced inflation, though the continuing provision of some poor relief (see above) may have alleviated some difficulties. The scarcity of coins within the town from 1645 onwards may also have made trading difficult until the final siege halted the flow of produce into the town. The parish registers show no evidence of increased mortality due to famine or dearth (though plenty due to infection), suggesting that generally the market was able to meet the basic needs of the town for most of the war.

Throughout the years 1642 to 1646, the town of Newark appears to have continued its role as an administrative and service centre for much of the region. Physicians based in the town or at the garrison provided their services to the inhabitants of surrounding villages. A couple of stray entries in the Upton Constable accounts for 1645 testify to this continued arrangement.

Spent with Mr Snales the surgeon one day when
he came to dresse John Kirkby

Earlier in the same year the constable had recorded 'my charges when I carried money to the surgions at Newark, May 3rd - 8d'.[220] There seems little reason to doubt that other service facilities in Newark continued to function throughout much of the war. In the absence of Quarter Sessions a 'Council of War' based at the Newark garrison appears to have administered a form of military justice. When soldiers from the Newark garrison killed William Robinson of Upton, it was to this council that the village constables turned for the administration of justice.

> Spent at Newark when I went with the soldiers that
> killed William Robinson. 10d.
> My charges the next day when I went with his
> wife and witnesses. 1s.[221]

Unfortunately the minutes of this council of war do not survive and so the outcome of this trial and evidence of how justice was administered are not available. The necessity to maintain law and order, and the fact that a small amount of material survives to suggest that this was achieved, testifies to the efficiency of this military provision. The question of its popularity, however, may be a different matter, and there is no way for us to gauge popular responses to this innovation.

In spite of the hardships of war, surviving records of the town testify to the continuation of civic ceremonial and local government. The provision of education, maintenance of public order, and the dignity of ceremonial events all figure in the surviving papers of this period. Salaries were often overdue and appointments delayed, but there appears never to have been any question of them not being met. For a period when so much evidence has disappeared, it is significant that details of such payments have survived. Officers appointed by the Corporation continued to be provided with their livery as witnessed by an order issued by the mayor on 5 December 1644

> You are hereby desired to deliver unto this bearer Richard
> Harper Gaoler, soe much broad cloth as shal be required for the
> making of him and the two serjeants of mace, cloakes according
> to custome.[222]

In fact, receipts survive from the years 1642 and 1644-1647 for the provision of the distinct 'blew broad cloth' used for making the Corporation livery. Despite siege, famine and dearth, the production of this dyed cloth and its manufacture into cloaks and gowns continued unabated. The insignia of office and authority likewise continued to be provided even though, at the town's surrender in 1646, the Corporation was forced to sell a considerable amount of plate and precious metal to raise capital.[223] A bill dated 15 February 1644(5) ordered

> These are to will and require you to pay unto Thomas Dixon
> the sume of twenty shillings due unto him for making twenty
> and one constable's staves.[224]

Even in the midst of war the dignity of office could not be compromised lest it lead to a further breakdown of order.

The remuneration of many of the town's officials and servants was often met from the rents received from lands gifted to the Corporation. As the war developed the collection of rents from lands lying distant from the town became increasingly difficult meaning that revenue was considerably reduced. Prior to 1640 the survival of bills of payment for wages is not uncommon, but after 1643 they diminish in number. Those that do survive show that wages and stipends had priority on expenditure, but that payment was frequently in arrears. The church organist and his six choristers were paid £6.5s per quarter from the Magnus rents prior to the war and although payment details survive for 1642, 1643 and 1645 thereafter they disappear altogether.[225] During the period of the Commonwealth such musical provision in a church would have been viewed as inclining towards Catholicism and, as such, was prohibited. This coupled with the dismantling of the organ prior to the town's surrender probably explains their absence from the records for the latter 1640s and throughout the 1650s.[226]

Over the period of the war considerable effort was exerted in guaranteeing the continuation of the Grammar School. Masters were appointed and kept in place throughout, and their stipend allowance of £20 per annum was paid quarterly in advance from the Magnus rents.

Table 5.3: Masters of the Newark Grammar School, 1642-1660

Name of Master	Period of Service
Richard Halliwell	c1639-1643
John Shore	1643-1649
Thomas Gibson	1649-1650
George Hill	1650-1655
Benjamin Masters	1656-1659

Records of stipend payments survive for 1643 and 1645 but by 1647, John Shore was being paid in arrears for at least two quarters.[227] During the final siege it appears that the Master's house had been damaged and that alternative accommodation had to be rented for Thomas Gibson in 1650.[228] By 1649 payments of the Master's stipends had reverted from quarterly to half yearly, possibly in arrears, probably in order to cope with limited finances and problems with cash flow.

The accounts of the constables and the Magnus rental accounts, both of which survive for 1645, illustrate the efforts made to maintain the pre war regime. The vicar was paid his 'Plow Monday Sermon' fee of £1.6s.8d, the Town Clerk Mr Martin his £4 per annum allowance, and the two 'serjeants of mace' their £3 per annum salary.[229] Money may well have been scarce, but good public order was essential if the town was to survive and this could only be guaranteed by keeping its officials in place and suitably remunerated.

Amid the social, economic and military disruptions of the Civil War period, everyday life within the town of Newark observed a regularity and continuity that illustrates amply the resilience of both local government and ordinary citizens. Civic and ecclesiastical offices continued to be filled and their holders were provided with their respective liveries - even if their wages were sometimes paid several months in arrears. Apart from the time of the final siege (November 1645-May 1646), the Corporation continued to collect the rents from its properties and lands in the vicinity of the town and used these for the charitable endowments they were originally given. The running of the Grammar School and Song School and the provision of accommodation for widows and poor relief for those in need continued to be met with varying degrees of success. Surviving poor rate accounts show that the amounts of money realised from the Book of Assessment were considerably reduced as poverty led many payers to default. As a result the war year accounts always operate at a deficit and how these shortfalls were made up is unclear. Yet in spite of all these real economic difficulties, it does appear that poor rate payments continued throughout the war.

The Civil War, whilst causing considerable hardships and periods of high mortality, did little to disrupt the basic human imperative to find a partner and raise a family. Decennial average marriage rates for the 1640s show an increase of around 16 per cent over those of the 1630s. In many ways this is to be expected as a consequence of the number of people moving into the town once the fighting began. This influx combined with the soldiers at the garrison, led to at least a doubling if not a trebling of the town's population. Both 1644 and 1646 witnessed numbers of marriages that were in excess of 50 per cent of the decennial average. A similar pattern may be discerned in the record of baptisms within the town. Throughout most of the 1640s and 1650s an average of around 80 baptisms per year was the norm but the figures for 1643-1645 witnessed a doubling of that rate.

Despite the material, economic, demographic and emotional difficulties of the Civil War period, the ordinary citizens and their rulers strove to maintain a degree of normality in community life. It was their self-sacrifice and sheer determination that provided the basis of continuity in the town during this vexatious period. As the contemporary commentator stated at the beginning of this chapter 'what is the city, but the people'.

CHAPTER 6

'The People of England...shall henceforth be governed as a Commonwealth and free state':[230]
Newark in the 1650s

Following the surrender of the Newark garrison in May 1646 it became important to preserve any social stability that remained in the town. The raging of plague until the start of 1647, poor harvests and grain shortages in 1647 and 1648 and the outbreak of a brief second Civil War in 1648 made it essential for the administrative life in the town to continue as undisturbed as possible. There was therefore no immediate purge of aldermen by the victorious Parliamentarians, even though a number of them had been identified as delinquents (see table 6.1). By 1650, however, the situation had changed considerably and the new republican authorities could turn their attentions to this former Royalist bastion with impunity.

On 30 January 1649, Charles I was executed outside the Banqueting House in Whitehall. England, Wales and Ireland were later declared to be 'a commonwealth and free state'. Not long afterwards, Abel Richardson surveyed the Manor of Newark (which had formerly belonged to the Crown) in order that it might be sold by Parliament. In spite of these uncertainties about ownership, control of transfers of land between freeholders and copyholders appears to have continued as usual. In other areas, however, the sale of the manor resulted in more serious consequences - for instance in the way local bridges were repaired and maintained. Possession of the manor guaranteed the receipt of certain bridge tolls but also involved the responsibility of on-going maintenance. Two local bridges in particular had suffered extensive damage during the fighting of the first Civil War; Kelham and Muskham, the latter being all but destroyed. No individual would take responsibility for the cost of these repairs and potential buyers for all or part of the manor sought exemption from these charges. Not until 3 September 1651 do we find that

> William Willoughby of South Muskham, Esq. did this day in open
> court promise and acknowledge himself that in his own right he would
> beare half the charge of the building of Muskham bridge, which the
> country who are consent to beare the other half in regard it was
> broken downe in time of warre.[231]

Whilst a compromise had been reached over the bridge at Muskham, the repairs at Kelham took longer to resolve. Extensive litigation was begun against Robert Sutton of Averham which dragged on in the courts right through until 1657. For the people of Newark these delays in the repairs to its major bridges not only caused inconvenience but also a considerable disruption to the re-establishment of trade in the town. At the Restoration in 1660, the Corporation of Newark petitioned the crown for the right to take control of both the collection of bridge tolls and their repairs, so as to avoid such chaos and disruption occurring again.[232]

The civic government of Newark experienced a major upheaval at the start of the 1650s as a consequence of the national execution of two Parliamentary ordinances. The first had originally been passed on 4 October 1647 and debarred all delinquents (former Royalists) from civic office, stripping them even of the right to participate in the election of local officials. The second, passed on 10 September 1649, required an oath to be sworn by all office holders to 'be true and faithful to the Commonwealth of England as it is now established without King or Lords'.[233] Aldermen who had formerly been supportive or sympathetic to the Royalist cause were now to be removed - either by coercion or conscience - from the corporation. In September 1650, the Newark Corporation met to discuss this ordinance and, consequently, the government of the town teetered on the brink of collapse. Of the twelve aldermen and the mayor, one had died and another had moved away: a further nine, including the mayor, tendered their resignation. Only Christopher Wilson and Robert Wilson were willing to continue to serve on the Corporation. The nine members who had tended their resignation were all technically debarred from office by the enforcement of the ordinance (see table 6.1) but the necessity of administrative continuity meant that only the resignations of five of the most prominent Royalist sympathisers were accepted. These were Edward Standish, Thomas Hancke, William Baker, John Marris and John Queningborough.[234] Between them they had served the Corporation for over 42 years and had managed to keep the town functioning throughout the worst of the Civil War. Both Standish and Baker had served as mayor during the Civil War and had worked closely with the Royalist garrison.[235] The resignations of the current mayor, William Watson, and aldermen John Johnson, Henry Cam and William Martin were not accepted. Johnson had actually borne arms for the King and both he and Cam had loaned money to the Royalist cause. What all this probably indicates is that the need for stable, effective government in the town was greater than the pressure central authorities could bring to bear upon the actions of the Corporation. Where those with experience could accommodate themselves to work within the new regime, their past indiscretions were overlooked and their talents used. This appears to have been a trend that was repeated in a number of former Royalist towns. After the surrender of Worcester in 1646 prominent Royalists were removed from the town corporation, such as the former Lieutenant General of the militia, but the need for a degree of stability in the town's economic recovery meant that the majority were not too closely scrutinised. As in Newark, it was not until after 1649 that a serious reorganisation of the Corporation members was undertaken. Worcester's involvement in the third Civil War of 1651 meant that further purging of the Corporation occurred in the 1650s, which was not the case in Newark. The former Royalist headquarters of Oxford seems to have presented a similar pattern of reforming its local government.[236] Until substantial further studies are undertaken, however, it is not possible to state whether this was a nationwide phenomenon.

Of the six individuals brought on to Newark's Corporation to make up its full compliment in 1650, only two men were complete newcomers to local politics. Yet even these two were men of considerable status and wealth, with Francis Fitzwilliam being described as a gentleman in the 1641 Subsidy, and Matthew Newham being able to bequeath £1100 in cash in his will of 1685.[237] Their appointment to the Corporation suggests both their acceptability to the new republican authorities and a willingness to work with the continuing aldermen. The other four appointees had all formerly been coadjutors, two of whom also had close links with the Royalists during the war. Thus even during the 1650s, town government remained in the hands of some of those men who had supported the king and generally the surviving minutes suggest that there was as considerable degree of co-operation with those newcomers to the Corporation.

Table 6.1 Individuals who supported the king and served in office after the surrender of Newark in 1646[238]

Individual	Bore arms?	Loan to king in war	Compounding Fine	Years served in office
Thomas Atkinson	Yes		£268*	1639-1650
William Baker		£150	£180	1644-1650
Francis Browne	Yes			1649-1650
Henry Cam		£100	£51.18s.*	1644-1650
Thomas Hancke		£75		1639-1650
Christopher Haslum			£100.17s.	1660-1673
William Hobman			£31.3s.4d.	1650-1659
Robert Hoys	Yes	£40		1662-1675
John Johnson	Yes	£840	£341.9s.8d.	1636-1660
John Marris	Yes			1646-1650
John Martin	Yes	£100	£37.6s.8d.	1657-1658
William Martin			£35.14s.4d.	1646-1662
John Queningborough			£40	1648-1650
Thomas Smith		£90		1641-1648
Edward Standish		£100	£539.10s.	1629-1650
Lancelot Thompson	Yes			1631-1649
George Wells			£40	CA 1646-1663

* = Fine later reduced   CA = Coadjutor

Despite such a situation of consent and co-operation between former Royalists and the new governors there was undoubtedly a line beyond which the central authorities would not allow the Corporation to pass. When, in 1651, the latter had the audacity to put forward the name of John Johnson as the next Mayor they were promptly overruled. Johnson's Royalist past was simply too well known for this appointment to be allowed. Elsewhere, events such as the proclamation of Charles II as King in Scotland caused the republican authorities to fear an invasion from the north, and anyone in England with a Royalist past was viewed with utmost suspicion. By 1657, however, the Corporation felt confident enough to put Johnson forward again as mayor, with the support of nine of the ten votes cast. This time he was successful, suggesting a growing resurgence of the former Royalists on the Corporation, and also a more stable polity at the centre of national government.[239]

The surviving minutes suggest that only one member of the Corporation spoke against this development. After February 1658, Francis Fitzwilliam began to absent himself from all council meetings saying, when challenged that he would not have 'anything to doe with those gentlemen who had come to act in the company against the acts of Parliamente or to this effect'.[240] Apart from this one episode, there remains little evidence of any great support for the republican regime amongst Newark's civic leaders throughout the 1650s. Christopher Wilson, indeed, took up many wider county responsibilities during the 1650s, including serving as a commissioner for the ejection of 'scandalous ministers' and also as a member of the Committee for the 'relief of creditors and poor prisoners' – this in spite of having served the town during its time as a Royalist garrison, loaned money to the king's cause and having his house damaged during the Parliamentarian bombardment. He was thus far from being a zealous republican.[241] The prevailing ethos of the Corporation during the 1650s appears to have been a desire for the well being of the town rather than any ideological commitment to the new regime.

Evidence for how the Corporation functioned is very scarce for the 1650s. Of the hundreds of Borough miscellaneous papers that survive from the seventeenth century only one comes from the 1650s. This is dated the 24 December 1650 and records the expenditure of £3.3s.8d in defence of a case being pursued through the Exchequer. No details are provided about the case and we are left to wonder what was so important for the town to expend such sums at a time when money was extremely tight.[242] It almost appears as if all the documentation produced over this decade has been carefully removed so as to wipe away any record. Thankfully brief notes are made in the Corporation minute book for the 1650s, though these are far from detailed. We have already explored what the minute book has to say about the changing personnel of the council, but there is more information that sheds light on other areas of town administration. Fire, for instance, was a constant concern of the town authorities (especially as so many buildings were constructed of timber) and on the 20 October 1655 they issued an Ordinance for a curfew during the winter months, in order to lessen the risk.

> An Ordinance for ye shuttinge of ye shops at seaven of ye clock at
> night from ye 1 of November until ye 25th of March... Ye curfew will
> be signalled by ye ringing of ye bell.[243]

Likewise, in the same year, they issued an Ordinance instructing shops not to sell goods on the Lord's day and also 'not to sell until the end of the sermon or other publique and godly services of these [week]dayes be finished'.[244]

Other tantalising references contained in the minute book show the Corporation continuing to appoint local officers to their posts throughout the 1650s. On the feast of St Nicholas in 1659, for instance, the aldermen agreed the selection of Mr Edward Leedes as the new town schoolmaster; In 1651 they agreed to the appointment of Mr William Landen as the deputy recorder to 'colonell John Hutchinson'.[245] The Corporation therefore continued to enjoy a degree of autonomy in running town affairs, in spite of the dubious past affiliations of some of its members.

The Quarter Session minutes for Nottinghamshire also survive for the 1650s and they too give us a glimpse of what was happening in Newark over this decade. Sabbath observance, for instance, was strictly enforced through the legal courts and this is explored fully in the next chapter. An interesting concern that came to the attention of the magistrates, meanwhile, was the number of guns in the possession of people in Newark and the surrounding areas. It may well be that these were a left over from the Civil War of the previous decade. The minutes noted that

> Severall complaints have been made of the great number of persons
> ...that keepe & shot in gunns contrary to the forme of divers laws
> and statutes of the Commonwealth & alsoe thereby neglecting to follow
> their callings to the Impoverishment of themselves & familys which may in
> time put them upon desperate courses to the disturbance of the public peace'[246]

As a potential threat to the public peace the justices issued an Order for 'the suppression of those that shoot with guns'. This would have been a concern to the justices in any period, but with so many former Royalists in and around the town there was a real concern that they might use their firearms to create further unrest. It was also in the interest of the justices to control the buying and selling of grain across the county if the public peace was to be kept. Therefore only licensed individuals, known as Badgers could undertake this trade. A Badger was required to be a married man, a householder, and over 30 years of age. A large amount of grain travelled up and down the river Trent and through Newark and so it is not surprising to find townsmen appointed to such roles over the decade. On the 8 January 1656 Thomas Harrison and John Maslland of Newark, both described as gentlemen, became licensed Badgers, and two years later, on the 14 July 1658, Robert Bailey, also described as a gentlemen, was similarly licensed. This is a useful insight as to the importance of Newark in the grain trade in Nottinghamshire, and beyond.

The relationship between the Corporation and the republican authorities in the county and nationally is hard to quantify owing to the scarcity of surviving evidence. Newark's proximity to the home of Major General Whalley at Screveton meant that he regularly visited the town, especially during the regime of the Major Generals between 1655 and 1656, and would have enjoyed a working relationship with the mayor and aldermen. Whalley was probably instrumental in bringing the Independent minister John James to preach in the town during the 1650s, though the Corporation also agreed to this.[247] On the death of Oliver Cromwell in 1658, the Corporation sent a loyal address to his son Richard promising him 'ready and cheerful obedience', though this may have been a matter of duty rather than enthusiasm.[248] Yet there was also a sense of relief across the country that the new leader was neither tainted by involvement in the regicide nor had any connection with the army. There was a popular belief that his government could mark a return to some form of normality.[249]

At the county sessions on 6 April 1657 there was a complaint by the county treasurers that

> The towne of Newarke hath neglected to pay their due Rates to the
> said Treasurers towards the relief of meighemed soldiers and widdowes
> and orphans of men slayne in ye late warre of this Commonwealth
> being £1.5s.4d yearly ever since ye year 1646 to ye great wronge of
> ye county and hindrance of ye public service.[250]

This levy was for the relief of those whose need was created because of their service to the Commonwealth - former Royalist soldiers and their relatives received none of this aid. Within Newark itself there were few, if any former Parliamentarians, but numerous needy former Royalists; there would have been little desire to reward one's former foes at the expense of the town's poor. The fact that the town was able to avoid paying the levy for over ten years is itself a testimony to the poor administration and lack of coercive power possessed by the county authorities. In 1657 this oversight was addressed, probably at the instigation of Major General Whalley, and Newark found itself with a retrospective bill of £15.4s. As this episode suggests, therefore, the town of Newark appears to have been far from being compliant with the new regime.

After the chaos of the 1640s, the 1650s saw a stabilising of food prices and slow economic improvement. The regime of Cromwell was blessed with a series of good harvests, with the years 1652-1655 being especially abundant. This may partly explain the appointment of additional Badgers in Newark in 1656 as mentioned above. From 1658 onwards, however, a run of bad harvests occurred nationally resulting in a dearth of grain over the years 1661-1662. This proved to be not the most auspicious start to the Restoration of Charles II in 1660.[251] The effects of these developments are reflected in the pages of the parish registers.

Table 6.2 Burials and Baptisms, 1650-1660

Year	Total children's burials	Total adult burials	Stranger burials recorded	Soldier burials recorded	Year total of burials	Annual total of baptisms
1650	20	16	-	-	36	52
1651	22	21	-	-	43	56
1652	8	5	-	1	14	54
1653	-	-	-	-	-	41
1654	36	40	-	-	76	95
1655	85	34	2	-	119	90
1656	33	45	4	1	78	111
1657	42	54	2	-	97	92
1658	55	72	3	1	127	86
1659	38	47	2	-	85	95
1660	42	55	3	-	97	95
Average	41.5	42.6			84.2	79

For Newark, the years 1650-1654 proved to be a period of low mortality and reduced fertility (see table 6.2). The combination of plague and famine at the end of the 1640s appears to have reduced the number of weak and vulnerable individuals and the number of marriages for 1647-1649 was considerably less than the decennial average (see Chapter 5). As a consequence the number of burials and baptisms recorded for these early years of the 1650s was very low, even allowing for the under-registration of burials in 1652 and the absence of records as the parish moved to civil registration in 1653. Whilst the number of baptisms recorded throughout the 1650s rises in 1654 and generally remains around the same figure for the rest of the decade, burial figures rise considerably around the same time and continue to increase thereafter.

In 1655 there was a devastating rise in the number of child burials with 85 being recorded. This was double the decennial average of 41.5 and was only just below the total of number children baptised in that year. The distribution of these deaths throughout the year shows a noticeable increase in the numbers for late spring and summer months, possibly suggesting an outbreak of childhood fever. Adult burials for the year are less than the decennial average showing that this was a childhood mortality crisis rather than one felt generally across the population. Some of the ground lost by this epidemic was restored the following year when the register records 111 baptisms, 33 more than the number of burials.

Throughout the 1650s a total of 772 burials against 867 baptisms was recorded. Allowance needs to be made for the fact that no burials were recorded in 1653 and there appears to have been considerable under-registration of deaths in 1652. If we substitute the figures of 14 and 0 with the decennial average of burials for the 1650s we arrive at a total of 926 deaths, giving an excess of burials over baptisms of 52. What the figures for the decade suggest, therefore, is that, at best, the population of the town remained static but more probably slightly decreased. Whilst this was in no way a general mortality crisis, the figures do suggest that the 1650s saw Newark make little headway in restoring its population to pre-Civil War levels.

The years 1657-1662 saw declining national harvests and Newark's experience of this catastrophe is writ large in its parish registers. For each of these years the annual adult burial totals exceeded the decennial average, with 1658 being a particularly severe year. The same picture is also conveyed through the children's burial totals, although 1659 proved to be an exception. The number of homeless people passing through Newark over much of this period suggests that these conditions were universal. We only discern their presence because some of them fell ill and died whilst passing through the parish with their burials in the churchyard being duly recorded. Even amongst the citizens of Newark an increasing number of those buried were identified as 'aged, widow or poor' suggesting that it was the most vulnerable who were succumbing to the increasing dearth. The seasonable distribution of burials suggests that mortality was at its worst when the shortage of food was most acute. Thus burials in the summer months are generally low with the majority being concentrated in the winter and early spring. For the ordinary citizens of Newark the hardships of the 1650s proved to be just as testing as the fighting and disease of the 1640s - a situation illustrated by the static nature of the town's population and its failure to recover both demographically and economically.

In 1653 the Barebones Parliament ordered that Civilian Registrars appointed by the local Justices of the Peace should undertake registrations of births (not baptisms), marriages and deaths.[252] In a number of parishes the parish clerk was appointed as Civil Registrar and this appears to have been the case in Newark for the registers display continuity of style throughout the decade. After 1653, for instance, the registers continue to record baptisms rather than births for the majority of entries, running entirely contrary to the instructions of the Ordinance. The difference may not be too significant for the above analysis of births for the 1650s because in the seventeenth century baptism occurred very soon after birth for children.

For the 1650s the average annual baptism/birth rate was 35 per cent less than that for the 1640s, yielding a figure of 79. This probably reflects the decrease in the number of people living within the town after the surrendering and dismantling of the garrison. It also reflects a slight decline in the size of the resident population as a result of mortalities in the 1640s (see Chapter 4). What the registers show very clearly is that only 19 per cent of annual baptisms occurred during the months June to August, with July being the quietest month. The majority of births appear to have taken place in the January to March quarter when a decennial average of 32 per cent was recorded. Conception rates within the town were still linked to the agricultural year, showing the importance of farming, and, in particular harvest time. The number of baptisms in 1653 (41) was particularly low for the decade but it is possible that this figure reflects the transition from parish to civil registration. As the decade progressed the birth rates increased with the years 1655-1660 yielding an average annual total of 94. In spite of growing economic difficulties and declining harvests the latter part of the 1650s saw an increasing birth rate. Unfortunately increasing mortality rates meant that the town's population failed to increase over this period.

As this chapter has shown, the 1650s were a period in which Newark attempted to set in place a recovery from the disastrous consequences of civil war. In spite of the many political developments at the centre of national government, within the town itself there appears to have been a degree of continuity both within local government and across everyday life. Some accommodation had to be arrived at with the new republican authorities and a few individuals with pronounced Royalist pasts were removed from office. Generally, however, there was a willingness to do as much as was necessary - but probably no more - to work with the new regime. For this very base level of co-operation there were to be severe repercussions after the Restoration of Charles II in 1660 when the new Royalist commissioners removed nine of the twelve aldermen from office.[253] They probably had little choice over the matter of co-operation in the 1650s for the parish registers suggest the presence of Parliamentarian soldiers in the town for most of the decade, with burials of soldiers being recorded in 1652, 1656 and 1658. Paradoxically, therefore, it appears that the town experienced greater outside interference in its daily activities after the Restoration than it ever did throughout the years of the Republic. Even so, there was popular rejoicing at the return of the king and the registers record six sons being christened with the name of Charles between May and September 1660; a name noticeably missing throughout the previous decade.

CHAPTER 7

**'Ad majorem Dei Gloriam':[254]
The life and worship of the
parish church, 1640-1660**

Standing at 236 feet the spire of St. Mary Magdalene dominates both the town and castle of Newark, and the wide flat meadows, which extend mile after mile along the river Trent. In the Civil War years it was the sheer physical presence of the church which served to remind the population of the pivotal nature of religion in their everyday lives. From the church tower the bells rang out announcing news, celebrating events, calling the faithful to prayer, and marking the hours of the day. In 1642, Charles Handley was paid 3s.4d 'for ringing 4 and 6 a clocke bell [and] tolling to prayers'.[255] The whole life of the community revolved around the ringing of the church bells. Up until 1646 the accounts refer to the first, second, third, forth and fifth bell. In 1646 there is a reference to a sixth or Great Bell, as there is again in 1656.[256]

The parish church of St. Mary Magdalene is one of the largest and finest of medieval churches in the country with an overall length of over 70 metres and a width of 40 metres. The manor and church at Newark-on-Trent had been granted to the Bishop of Lincoln in 1100 and the west tower of the present building was begun around 1220 with the side aisle being completed in 1312. The outbreak of the Black Death in 1349 halted building work and so the nave, north aisle, chancel and choir aisles were not completed until the second half of the fifteenth century. By this time Newark had become established as an important trading centre. Situated on the Great North Road where it crossed the river Trent it encouraged thriving wool-merchants and tradespeople to settle in the town. Discouraged by the bishop from endowing their own smaller churches, the various trade guilds put their efforts into endowing St. Mary Magdalene's with superb woodwork and stained glass. Originally each of these guilds had their own chapel in the church but these were removed at the Reformation. By the seventeenth century the decorated walls had largely been whitewashed, chantry chapels made obsolete, and Catholic elements of the decoration ejected. A large part of the medieval stained glass, however, remained in place and was to become one of the main victims of the Civil War in the 1640s.

This impressive medieval church was a prominent feature in the Trent valley, a source of civic pride to the town authorities and a central factor in the lives of the parishioners.[257]

The policy of William Laud, archbishop of Canterbury, to bring uniformity and beauty to the fabric and liturgy of the Church of England during the 1630s meant that by 1640 the parish church of Newark was in a better state of repair than it had been for decades. By July 1636, the communion table had been moved to the east end of the church and railed in, but not before the churchwardens had been excommunicated for lack of action.[258] Between 1636 and 1637 a further sum of £240 was expended on the fabric of the church. These works included the making of the seats 'seemly and uniform' and adding a further 50 or 60 seats for parishioners, and the re-paving of an estimated area of 3,200 square feet of the church floor.[259] Alongside these improvements greater adherence to the liturgy of the Prayer Book was observed and visits by the king on five separate occasions between 1636 and 1641 probably helped ensure liturgical conformity. Whatever the feelings of parishioners about such developments (no evidence survives) the parish church was clearly meeting the expectations of Laudian policy by the start of the Civil War.

The turbulent events of the 1640s and 1650s are all reflected in the churchwarden's accounts for this period. These, along with the Borough Council minutes, parishioner wills and the Quarter Session records (where they survive) provide us with an in-depth insight to parochial life. Dividing the accounts for this twenty-year period into five distinct sections, this chapter will explore the events as they impinged upon church life. The five blocks will be the Prelude to War (1640-1641), the Civil War (1642-1646), Uncertain Peace (1647-1649), the New Regime (1650-1658) and the Road to Restoration (1659-1660). See also Table 7.1 below for a general summary of the accounts.[260]

Table 7:1 Churchwarden Account Details, 1640-1660

Year	Income	Extra Leys	Expenditure	Balance(+/-)
1640	£82.18s.10d.	3	£97.3s.6d.	-£14.4s.8d.
1641	£69.18s.6d.	2	£72.3s.3d.	-£2.4s.9d.
1642	£65.19s.0d.	2	£75.3s.9d.	- £9.4s.9d.
1643	£66.9s.10d.	1	£79.0s.2d.	- £12.10s.4d
1644	£75.18s.4d.	1	£79.9s.6d.	- £3.11s.2d.
1645	£68.1s.10d.	1	£67.14s.1d.	+ 7s.9d.
1646	£65.1s.7d.	0	£69.13s.9d.	- £4.12s.2d.
1647	£46.7s.7d.	1	£48.18s.10d.	- £2.11s.3d.
1648	£49.1s.10d.	1	£54.18s.2d.	- £5.16s.4d.
1649	£47.16s.1d.	1	£48.17s.4d.	- £1.1s.3d.
1650	£42.10s.8d.	1	£40.10s.5d.	+ £2.0s.1d.
1651	£58.6s.8d.	1	£59.3s.2d.	- 16s.6d.
1652	£56.6s.0d.	2	£54.1s.0d.	+ £2.5s.0d.
1653	£59.12s.8d.	2	£60.19s.3d.	- £1.6s.7d.
1654	£53.6s.8d.	2	£56.11s.3d.	- £3.4s.7d.
1655	£57.3s.5d.	2	£54.2s.1d.	+ £3.1s.4d.
1656	£49.8s.11d.	1	£45.9s.2d.	+ £3.19s.9d.
1657	£49.13s.1d.	1	£50.6s.2d.	-13s.1d.
1658	£55.1s.6d.	2	£57.15s.10d.	-£2.14s.4d.
1659	£57.9s.5d.	2	£58.17s.10d.	-£1.8s.5d.
1660	£95.12s.0d.	3	£115.9s.3d.	-£19.17s.3d.

Prelude to War, 1640-1641

By 1640 the consequence of Laudian reform had reached its zenith in Newark, but the road to hostilities between king and Parliament was marked by the ongoing financial burden which these innovations had placed on the parish. In 1640, three additional leys had to be raised to meet both the inherited debt from 1639 and the projected expenditure for the current year. Even with this additional income the churchwardens still had to hand over to their successors a deficit of £14.4s.8d. Although the furnishings of the church now met Laudian requirements the fabric of the church still fell short of the authorities' ideal of 'beauty of holiness'. The sum of £13.17s.10d was spent on repairing and weather proofing the church windows, a substantial outlay that, within three years, was to be undone as a result of siege and bombardment. For all this work the wardens had to appear before the ecclesiastical court to certify their completion, incurring further fees and expenses amounting to £1.14s. By the end of 1641 the wardens were beginning to clear the debts of refurbishment with the help of a further two additional leys. By the outbreak of hostilities the debt had been reduced to just £2.4s.9d but further financial improvement was to be curtailed by the expense of the war.

The deteriorating political situation is referred to in the accounts. In 1641 three fasts were held in the parish to pray for the degenerating national situation with 3s.4d being spent on the relevant liturgical books. The king's presence in and around Newark, following his exit from London, is noted in both 1640 and 1641 with the bell ringers being paid to announce both his arrival and departures. In 1640 four of the town's inhabitants were paid 2s to 'watch the king's goods'. In spite of the uncertainty of the times the warden's accounts testify to the continuity of parish life, with routine maintenance and regular worship expenses being met. Within Newark, the parish church appeared to provide the stability that national politics seemed to be undermining across the country. The presence of the king and the regular outlay of money that this required seem to suggest that already there was a strong strand of Royalism within the town. The great theological debates about the nature of church and state that were endemic across the country do not appear to have impinged upon the parochial life of St. Mary Magdalene's in Newark. The Civil War formally began with the raising of the royal standard at Nottingham Castle on 24 August 1642, but in reality preparations had begun much earlier in the year. For the next four years, the parish and town of Newark were at the very centre of events. Newark's status as a maiden Royalist garrison until its surrender in May 1646 probably explains why the daily life and liturgy of the church remained unchanged but there were to be other costs which bit deep into the life of the parishioners.

The Civil War (1642-1646)

An immediate consequence of Civil War was a large increase in the size of Newark's population. The establishment of a garrison and the arrival of local Royalist supporters with their families probably trebled the number of inhabitants. For the parish church this would have had an immediate effect on the practice of worship and the provision of church consumables. In 1641 the amount spent on providing wine for communion services amounted to £11.1d but by 1643 this figure had risen to £18.11s.9d and the following year to £20. With the ending of hostilities in 1646 and the disbanding of the garrison the sum for 1647 plummeted to £5.11s.8d. Obviously greater numbers were attending the services and this in turn placed greater wear and tear on church furnishings. A similar pattern may be discerned in the fees received for burials, which in 1641 amounted to £12.2s.11d but by 1644 had risen to £33.7s.9d. The frequent outbreak of typhus and later plague (see chapter 5) contributed greatly to this vast increase (just over 170 per cent) but was not the sole factor: an increase in population usually equates to greater numbers of deaths. In the years 1643 and 1644, the annual expenditure of the churchwardens exceeded £79, a sum not to be surpassed until the Restoration of Charles II in 1660. These two years witnessed a deficit of £12.10s.4d and £3.11s.2d respectively. In 1645 expenditure had been reduced to £67 and for the only time over the period of the war the accounts were to show a surplus of 7s.9d. Throughout the years 1642-1646 a large percentage of the expenditure went on the church fabric, with £5.13s.4d being spent on the church leads in 1642, just as the war began. Whereas under archbishop Laud large sums were spent on beautifying the church, once the war began most of the money went on repair and renewal of war-damaged fabric. Ironically though, war proved to be a cheaper option for church fabric than Laudian reform.

Throughout the vicissitudes of war it was the parish church, with its continuity of liturgy and calendar, that provided a sense of stability for the town's citizens. In 1642 18s was spent on repairing the church Prayer books and bible and within 12 months additional copies of the prayer book were purchased from a bookbinder in Lincoln for the sum of 11s. Although an Ordinance of Parliament abolished the Prayer Book in January 1645[261] , it continued to be used in Newark until after the surrender of the town in May 1646. Thereafter the churchwardens were compelled to purchase the *Directory of Worship* and use it in place of the Prayer Book. In a world of uncertainty and change, the worship life of St. Mary Magdalene's provided a familiar point of reference for parishioners. Money continued to be spent on the furnishings of worship (albeit at a reduced rate); the pulpit was repaired and painted in 1645 and 1646, and a new hood was made for the vicar in 1643 at a cost of £1.6s.8d. The increase in the number of worshippers necessitated the purchased of two additional pewter flagons for 10s.6d. in 1645. The increasing number of burials also required the construction of an additional bier in 1643 and both of them required repairing at the start of 1646. As far as possible the wardens sought to maintain parish community life. The perambulation was held in 1642, 1643, and 1644 and again in 1646, although by then it was a considerably reduced affair, possibly because of plague and siege. Usually around £2.9s.3d was spent on the perambulation but in 1646 only 7d was spent. It appears that war and disease made the event impossible in 1645. In the face of overwhelming odds heroic action was exerted in maintaining parochial and community life.

The fabric of the church appears to have suffered considerably over the course of the war and the town's three sieges. Much of the damage remained unaddressed until after the war had ended with the largest sums of money being spent in 1647, 1648 and 1649 (see below). The windows, upon which so much money had been expended in 1640, had a further £1.14s.6d spent on them after the siege of 1644. Thereafter they were generally neglected until the end of hostilities. In 1645, however, Richard Symonds still found himself impressed by what he saw of them

> North yle, church window, divers coates, especially the coates of
> Leake both with and without a border...In the south window,
> the crosse yle, church, in very old glasse, towards the bottome,
> these following, and in this manner fairely depicted in six
> severall panes: the sheild of Deyncourt four times
> in every pain.[262]

When the town finally surrendered most of the medieval glass that had survived both the Reformation and the bombardment of three sieges, was deliberately destroyed by puritan iconoclasts and only fragments of original glass now survive in the south east chapel. Emergency repairs to the church roof at the surrender of the town in May 1646 may suggest that a part of it had been previously stripped of lead in order to make musket balls for the besieged Royalist garrison. In the midst of plague and economic distress, £9.3s.3d had to be spent on new lead to make the church weatherproof. Again after the surrender money was spent on 'gathering up pinacles, lead, and glasse bettered down in ye siege'.

With the surrender of the garrison in 1646 much of the anti-Anglican legislation passed by Ordinance of Parliament could now be enforced within the town.

Familiar liturgies and furnishings were to be suddenly removed and the presence of Parliamentarian troops in the locality meant that there was little opportunity to avoid following the letter of the law. The church organ was the first victim of this new regime. In May 1646 it was hastily removed from the church at a cost to the wardens of 6s.6d. To Puritan reformers the organ was an 'instrument of the devil'; a popish survival in what should be a true reformed Protestant church. It was probably removed in order to protect it from vandalism and destruction by Parliamentarian soldiers. Surprisingly, the pulpit was also removed not long afterwards. Parliament sought to impose sound and godly preaching in every parish church of the land. This certainly happened in Newark, for in March 1647 the wardens recorded they had spent £6.8s.6d over the past 12 months in securing the services of preaching ministers. Although the vicar Henry Trueman was still in the living at this time, he was viewed with a degree of suspicion by the new authorities. He was removed from the living at Cromwell in 1650 and may have been suspended from Newark at the same time because of his known Royalist sympathies.[263] In the light of the Parliamentarian emphasis upon preaching it remains unclear why Newark's pulpit was removed. It may have been a last act of defiance by the vicar and wardens before the surrender to hinder Puritan preachers - or more likely the pulpit proved too ornate for Puritan taste.

Whilst pulpit and organ were removed, the sixteenth century rood screen appears to have been left in place and undamaged. At the same time as furnishings were being removed, soldiers were paid 1s to take Prayer Books, linen and flagons to the vicar's house for safe keeping. Officially Books of Common Prayer were supposed to be handed over to the authorities to be destroyed but in Newark at least some of them were kept and at the Restoration in 1660 5s had to be spent on repairing them. The surplices were washed for the last time in June 1646 and thereafter they disappear from the churchwarden's accounts until 1660. The sum of 1s.8d was spent in 1660 in fetching the remains of the old stone font back into the church from the churchyard and it is probable that this had been removed forcibly from the building by the Parliamentarian soldiers after the surrender of the town in 1646. It was certainly badly damaged and a new bowl had to be put on it at the Restoration. Finally a *Directory of Worship* was purchased for 2s in November 1646 and the transformation of liturgy and fabric was then complete. The continuity of the war years was now at an end and the parishioners faced an uncertain and innovative future at the church.

Uncertain Peace (1647-1649)

By the end of 1646 fighting had ended across most of England, though not in Wales and now began the vexed issue of finding an accommodation between the defeated Charles I and his Parliament. The pursuit of peace proved to be much more elusive than that of a military victory and in 1648 a smaller second Civil War erupted, which culminated in the execution of the king in January 1649. The surviving parish and corporation records make no mention of these unfolding national events, suggesting that the town of Newark was not involved in any major way. Close monitoring by local Parliamentarians, the aftermath of plague, and the dire economic circumstances conspired to ensure that the town was otherwise engaged. The most noticeable feature of the period 1647-1650 in Newark was the reduction of the number of people in the town. The dismantling of the Royalist garrison, plague, typhoid and the unwillingness of victorious Parliamentarians to establish a garrison in an infected town, combined to remove large numbers of people. During the war years the wardens spent on average £17.1s.7d per annum on providing wine for communion services. Between 1647 and 1650 this annual figure fell to £7.4s.10d. There is no evidence to suggest that sacrament services were reduced in number and the most likely explanation is that numbers attending were considerably reduced. Alongside this the average annual amount of fees for burials fell from £22.6s.11d to £5.17s.4d for the corresponding periods. These figures serve to emphasise the decline in the town's population.

The economic situation of the town was very fragile in the years following the war. Many parishioners had lent money to the Royalist cause and now had little chance of retrieving it. Alongside this was the extensive damage inflicted upon the town and church which now had to be repaired. The churchwarden's accounts reflect this financial hardship in their record of income and expenditure both of which were reduced on average by £20 per year (just under 33 per cent of the war budget). Yet even allowing for considerably reduced expenditure for three of the years between 1647-1650 there was a deficit in the accounts, with that of 1648 amounting to £5.16s.4d This was the largest sum for five years. In spite of considerable damage to the fabric of the church, repairs were carefully controlled so as not to raise more than one additional ley in any year. In 1647 the churchyard fence was replaced at a cost of £4.14s.10d. The original was probably dismantled during the harsh winter of 1645/46, to be used as firewood. Attention too was focussed on the roof when in 1648 and 1649 £4.7s.7d and £6.16s.1d were spent on leads and plumbers.

In 1648 £5.7d was spent on providing preaching ministers for the church, even though the vicar still held the living. The accounts and Corporation records clearly show that a small detachment of Parliamentarian soldiers was established in the town once the plague had gone[264]. These troops probably required the preaching services of clergyman more sympathetic to their cause than that of the vicar. Provisions for a preaching minister also appear in the accounts over this period. In 1650 an hourglass was purchased for 1s, the length of sermons could now be clearly monitored. In the same year £1.18s.5d was spent on altering the reading pew. The consequences of Parliamentarian Ordinances also begin to appear in the churchwarden's accounts. A 'basin for baptisme' was purchased for 4s in 1650, as the old stone font lay broken in the churchyard. The disruption of this period is conveyed in the number of people recorded as passing through the parish. In 1649, ten individuals with letters of request passed through the town and the wardens gave them a total of £1.7s.6d. This amount (about 2 per cent of the annual expenditure) was the largest payment for several decades. It appears that the wars had financially ruined and displaced a number of people around the country.

The New Regime (1650-1658)

The 1650s were to witness a closer co-operation between clergy and magistrates in creating a godly commonwealth across the realm. Fasts, sermons and the enforcement of Sabbath observance were prominent features of this policy and these were to greatly impinge upon the lives of Newark parishioners. On 11 January 1654, John Armstrong, Thomas Haslam, George Arnold and Steven Arnold, all of Newark, were indicted at the Quarter Sessions for 'tipling in an alehouse on the Lord's day'. Armstrong was fined 12d and the others 6d each for this breach of the Sabbath.[265] In the Borough Minutes of 1655 there is recorded an order for shopkeepers forbidding them to sell goods on the Sabbath and also not to trade in the week during the time of the 'sermon and other publique and godly services of those days'.[266]

The abolition of the ecclesiastical courts made the enforcement of religious conformity almost impossible and the Instrument of Government of 1653 rescinded compulsory attendance at one's parish church.[267] This new found religious freedom enabled Protestant dissenting congregations to form in many parishes across the country but surprisingly there is little evidence of such activity in Newark. In 1659 the Quaker William Dewsberry preached at two meetings in the town but these were violently disrupted by local inhabitants, urged on by some leading citizens.[268] The Quakers failed to become established in the town and by the time of the 1669 ecclesiastical census there were no nonconformist congregations recorded as meeting in Newark.[269] Just as the majority of the population remained loyal to the king in civil matters, so, even after military defeat, do they appear to have remained steadfast in their adherence to conservative religion and, as far as they could, Anglican practices.

The annual expenditure of the churchwardens over the period 1651-1658 remained around the £55 to £60 mark, apart from the year 1656 when it fell to £45.9s.2d (See table 7.1). Over this eight-year period, three years witnessed a surplus of income and a further two a deficit of only a few shillings. The total annual surpluses amounted to £9.6s.1d, whilst the deficits came to £8.14s.1d giving a net balance of 12s over the eight years. Annual fees received from burials increased by over a 100 per cent from those obtained over the years 1650-1652 and remained around £6.10s for the period 1653-1658. Whilst at face value these figures suggest a rise in mortality they may also testify to the gradual recovery of the town's population after the plague of 1646-1647. The mid 1650s witnessed a series of poor harvests (see Chapter 6) and this may also – at least in part – account for the increase in deaths.

Repairs to the war-damaged fabric of the parish church continued well into the 1650s. In 1651 the sum of £6.13s was spent on additional repairs to the roof and in 1653 a further £2.9s.6d was spent on the leads. In the previous year, meanwhile, £4.3s.4d had been spent on 'mending the church windows'. These repairs, however, did not complete the works for further expenditure was required in 1654 when £2.17s.6d was spent on the windows and again in 1657 when £5.2s.3d was spent on the leads. These figures represent between 4 and 10 per cent of the annual churchwarden's expenditure. The wooden fence around the vicarage probably suffered the same fate as the churchyard fence during the final winter siege of 1645-1646 (see above). The wardens, however, could not afford to replace it until 1651 when it cost £4.17s.4d. Plague, financial hardship and the lack of available money all contributed towards repairs to the church being spread over fully 9 years.

The number of burials during the years of high mortality caused problems to the church floor. In 1653, 1s.6d was spent on labourers 'raising settled gravestones in [the] church and choir' and a further 4s.8d was needed the following year for the same purpose. Further work on the gravestones had to be done in 1656 and 1657. There are no records of such activity in the accounts for the two decades prior to the 1650s.

The worship life of the church during the 1650s is also hinted at in the surviving accounts of the churchwardens. Days of thanksgiving and fasting ordered by the authorities were duly observed with the necessary purchase of liturgies and the ringing of church bells. A new Bible was purchased in 1653 at a cost of £1.10s and the fees paid to preaching ministers are also periodically recorded. A mid week lecture also appears to have been established in the town for in 1657 the accounts record payments to 'Mr James at his lectures for wine'. Beating the bounds of the parish at Rogation time (the perambulation) which had ceased in 1646 was revived in 1653 when £1.17s.4d was spent on bread, cake and ales. It continued thereafter throughout the 1650s. The sums spent in the 1650s appear to have been little different from that expended twenty years earlier suggesting that the activities remained largely the same.

The church bells continued to ring out on 5 November and on other occasions as prescribed by the new authorities and, together with the parish clock, began once again to figure prominently in the life of the community. In 1652, £4.10s was spent on mending the clock and chimes with a further £5.8s.11d being spent on them in 1658. The sum of £4 was spent on repairing the bells in 1654 with a further outlay of £10.14s.9d. being made in 1658. These sums represented a sizeable part of the annual outlay of the churchwardens in those respective years. Annually new ropes had to be shot up to the different bells, testifying to their regular usage in calling parishioners to worship and the observation of prescribed fasts and sermons.

In December 1644, Parliament had passed an Ordinance that sought to curtail celebrations connected with the feast of Christmas. Indeed, in many respects it sought to abolish Christmas altogether. The legislation stated

> that this day in particular is to be kept with the more solemn
> humiliation, because it may call to remembrance our sins, and
> the sins of our forefathers, who have turned this feast, pretending
> the memory of Christ, into an extreme forgetfulness of him, by
> giving liberty to carnal and sensual delights.[270]

Parliament sat on Christmas Day 1644 and shops in London were ordered to remain open as popular festivities and feasting were put down. Initially this unpopular legislation mainly affected London but with the winning of the war and further Ordinances in 1647 and 1652, by the mid 1650s it was applied across much of the country. Newark would have most certainly been affected with its popular celebrations being controlled. The memory of this time, however, appears to have been all but expunged from surviving records. Legislation about the opening times of the town's shops was recorded in the Borough minutes (see above) but there is no specific reference to how this applied at Christmas. There was probably no worship at St. Mary's on Christmas Day, as there had been previously, but there is no specific reference to this in the churchwarden's accounts. At London in 1653, John Evelyn wrote in his diary

> 25. Christmas-day no churches or publique Assembly, I was
> faine to pass the devotions of that blessed day with my family
> at home.[271]

The new authorities would have closely monitored a town with such a renowned Royalist past as Newark and anything that resembled opposition to the Republic would have been swiftly dealt with. Certainly during the tenure of Major General Edward Whalley as the regional military governor (1655-1657) Newark was under close scrutiny (see Chapter 6) and the popular festivities of Christmas would have been one of his targets.

The Lord Protector Oliver Cromwell died on 3 September 1658, plunging the country into a period of considerable political and religious uncertainty. Not until the Restoration of Charles II in May 1660 were many of the above Ordinances re-assessed and rescinded. The re-establishment of the monarchy in 1660 and the Anglican Church in 1662 created great expense for the churchwardens of Newark as church liturgies and furnishings were restored to their pre 1642 condition. The year 1659, often seen as a prelude to the Restoration, proved for Newark to be one of high mortality and considerable uncertainty.

The Road to Restoration (1659-1660)

The failure of Richard Cromwell, the army coup and the actions of General George Monck at the close of 1659 all helped to create a national air of uncertainty as people waited to see what would happen next.[272] During this period the Newark churchwarden's appear to have refrained from any major expenditure on the fabric or furnishings of the church. Necessary maintenance did continue but the only large sums of expenditure were £6.3s.8d on repairing the bells, £2.9s on the clock and chimes and £4.19s.2d on restoring the steeple, which had been damaged by canon fire in 1644. At the end of the financial year of 1659-1660, 166 bassacks were brought for the communion table and church for £2.5s. An inventory of 1661 recorded 160 'litle bassackes of one hight and six great ones for the communion table'.[273] It appears that by this time the parish officers sensed that the Puritan revolution had run its course and now was the time to move back towards a more Anglican style of worship. Although two additional leys were raised in 1659, the £8.18s.10d received in funeral fees (an increase of over 45 per cent on those of the previous year) helped cover most of the parish expenses leaving an end of year deficit of just £1.8s.5d, just under half that of the previous year.

It is in the accounts for 1660-1661 that we catch a glimpse of the full expense to the parish of restoring Anglican worship and, indirectly, the amount of destruction that had occurred over the previous decade. New pulpit cloths, communion cloths and silk cushions were purchased to adorn the church at a cost of £6.1s.5d. The royal coat of arms, whitewashed over after the execution of Charles I in 1649, were redrawn and repainted at the tremendous cost of £23.13s.4d. This represented over 20 per cent of the total parish expenditure for 1660. Those prayer books that had survived hidden away since 1646 were repaired at a cost of 5s and an additional six copies were purchased for the choir for £2.1s. The remains of the old stone font were carried into the church by a labourer who was paid 1s.8d. The font was found to be severely damaged and had to be 'rebuilt by the charity of Nicholas Ridley, 1660'.[274] As a consequence of this repair the fifteenth century figures of saints on the base of the font now have seventeenth century heads with beards and moustaches.[275] Once again civic pride in the parish church came to the fore and £2.12s.3d was spent on 'sweeping the pillars and church' so as to highlight the many improvements. In 1660 surplices appear again in church worship after an absence of 14 years with John Hilton being paid 9s to wash them.

The perambulation of 1660 proved to be an extravagant affair, a celebration not only of beating the parish boundary but also of the recent return of Charles II to London. Over the previous five years the annual average expenditure on this event had been £2.6s, although in 1659 the churchwardens had spent £3.11d. In 1660 the amount spent was a staggering £8.7s.11d, nearly a fourfold rise. The amount of ale and cakes consumed must have been considerable as the parish reaffirmed its Royalist sympathies and relief at the disbanding of the republican regime. The perambulation had occurred within a few days of the king's return to his capital and so it is easy to see how rogation and Restoration became combined in one event.

To finance these many ecclesiastical alterations the churchwardens were forced to raise three additional leys. This raised a total income of £95.12s, which was £36.14s.2d more than the total expenditure of 1659. Yet despite this large income (the highest for over 21 years) the end of the year witnessed a financial deficit of £19.17s.3d. This exceeded any other deficit over the period 1640-1659 and must have been reminiscent of the sorts of debts incurred during the Laudian reforms of the 1630s. To make matters worse, over the winter of 1660 a severe storm struck the town and caused considerable damage to the fabric of the church. This night of the 'great wind' added further expense to an account that was already in deficit.

The sum of £6.2s was spent about the leads and £2.5s.10d on 'the stone which was blown down'. Replacement wood and other repairs amounted to £3.6s and 10s had to be spent on erecting scaffolding to facilitate the repairs. In all, the storm caused £12.3s.10d worth of damage, an expense on an account already stretched. It is possible that this storm was the one referred to by Samuel Pepys in his diary entries for the 8 and 9 December 1660 when he noted that HMS Assurance sank with the loss of 20 lives.[276] In an age that believed in portents, omens and signs, this inauspicious start to the reign of Charles II may have caused a degree of alarm to some of Newark's inhabitants.

An interesting entry in the 1660 accounts records the payment of 2s.6d to the sexton, Richard Yoxall for 'keeping the church dores locct on Shrove Tuesday'. This most certainly refers to the year 1661 as the financial year did not end until Lady Day (25 March). During the 1650s, Puritans had attempted to curtail the popular celebrations of Shrove Tuesday by making it a solemn fast day to be observed in church. Prior to 1642, this day had been marked by 'eating, drinking and behavioural excess'[277] and with the Restoration there was a return to these age-old Shrove Tuesday festivities. It is possible, therefore, that in a spirit of release from the unpopular policies of the 1650s, the church doors were locked to *prevent* any form of worship!

At the end of the financial year 1659-1660 an inventory of church goods was taken by the churchwardens and recorded in the Coucher Book. The inventory reveals just how quickly the parish had returned to Anglican practices and the degree to which the church had managed to avoid compromising with the republican authorities. Amongst the books listed were a large reading Bible and a smaller Bible for the mayor's pew, the *Paraphrase of Erasmus* (2 volumes), Foxes *Book of Martyrs*, two large Prayer Books and four smaller Prayer Books. There were also listed four liturgies 'to be used in time of danger for the preservacon of his Majesties person' dated 1626, 1628, 1636 and 1640. These had obviously been kept hidden away from prying eyes during the Interregnum. New cushions, surplices for the vicar, organist and 6 choirboys and a 'new greene carpett foure yardes and a halfe long' for the communion table were also listed. To store the new furnishings there was a great chest and a 'box to keepe the cloathes in'. The sacramental life of the church was reflected in the ten pewter flagons for communion, 'a pewter bason for baptisme' (the stone font was still being repaired) and a new register book of velum. By the end of 1661 Anglicanism had been clearly re-established in Newark, nearly a year before the Act of Uniformity in 1662. Here more than anywhere else are we given an insight into the enduring conservative nature and Royalist sympathies of the town, or at least its leading citizens.

The 1640s and 1650s proved to be a period of considerable flux and change for the people of Newark. Although the new authorities strictly regulated parochial organisation after 1646, control of the spiritual life of its parishioners proved to be much more elusive. St. Mary Magdalene parish church was spared much of the iconoclasm that occurred in London churches and those in the Puritan stronghold of East Anglia.[278] With Newark garrisoned by Royalist troops until May 1646, and with plague raging in the town for twelve months thereafter, its surrender actually kept large numbers of Parliamentarian troops at bay until 1647. At the town's surrender the church authorities dismantled any furnishings that might be at risk of vandalism, and appear to have hidden them away in storage. Thus physical damage by religious reformers was kept to a minimum, although considerable damage had been caused by bombardment during the sieges of 1644 and 1645-46.

The richness and beauty of the worship experience was thus considerably diminished for the parishioners of Newark after 1646. The sacraments were stripped of much of their furnishings, liturgy and ceremonial, as font, communion rails, Prayer Book and surplices were removed in accordance with Parliamentarian Ordinance. During the 1650s baptisms and communion were celebrated simply and with little embellishment. A plain pewter basin was used for christenings and the liturgy of the Eucharist, now devoid of the rich prose of Cranmer, followed the simple Gospel narrative of the Lord's supper. Preaching services, accompanied by fasts or acts of thanksgiving, became the standard fare of church worship with godly preachers being brought into the town from neighbouring parishes.

The conservative nature of the town and its inhabitants could not be totally extinguished however. Although closely monitored, where possible long-established parochial activities were continued. The perambulation provides the clearest example of this, recommencing in 1653 and continuing throughout the rest of the decade. The ease with which the church moved back into Anglicanism after the Restoration of Charles II and the lack of nonconformist congregations in the town after 1660 all testify to the prevailing conservative nature of the town.[279] Prayer Book worship and ritual were well established at St Mary Magdalene church twelve months prior to the Act of Uniformity in 1662.

Although war, pestilence, economics and Puritan zeal had considerable short-term impact on the life of the church in Newark during the 1640s and 1650s, their long-term effect on the ethos and ambience of worship was minimal. Anglican liturgy, aligned to the seasons and popular custom, were too well established in the parishioner's psyche to be permanently suppressed. The sheer physical presence of the large medieval church was a visible reminder of a spiritual tradition that was even more firmly established.

EPILOGUE

The position of Newark upon Trent, situated on the Great North Road at the lowest crossing point on the river Trent, meant that it was always going to be of strategic importance once the war began. The survival, even to this day, of extensive earthworks and fortifications is visible proof of the military activity that went in to defending and besieging it over a four year period. Coupled with these physical remains there also exists a number of military accounts of actions that occurred in and around the town. Together, these sources have ensured that the military story of Newark has been often told. By contrast, this volume has told another story: the testimony of the ordinary men, women and children, who through no fault of their own, found themselves caught up in the momentous events that unfolded around them. Their own political, religious and economic inclinations were rarely recorded and often ignored, but the demographic, economic and social consequences of the war were very real for them.

The presence of large numbers of soldiers, both in and around the town had dramatic consequences for the inhabitants. Overcrowding within the town placed considerable pressures on both the availability of resources and the number of people living in a building. Such conditions were ideal for the spread of disease and malnutrition and, in an age that was familiar with periodic mortality crises, the consequences for Newark were still shocking. The three typhus epidemics over the period 1643-1646 probably killed between 12 and 15 per cent of the town's civilian population, and when combined with the numbers who died of plague in 1646, may account for the overall demise of between 25 and 30 per cent of the population. For the survivors these bald figures hide a raft very real personal consequences wherein family, friends, life-long neighbours and, for the younger citizens, potential marriage partners were all taken from them. Not until the end of the eighteenth century was Newark to enjoy a demographic upturn that was to reverse the consequences of the Civil War period.

Alongside this very human cost of war there were also the financial consequences engendered by the destruction of property. The need to build defensive ramparts and ditches meant the clearing away of large amounts of property. Some of the timber framed buildings could be dismantled and re-assembled in other places, but space within the defences became increasingly scarce as the war progressed. Those buildings that were damaged or destroyed during the three sieges were not so fortunate, and the lack of finance and limited availability of materials meant that most were not rebuilt or repaired for many years. Even as late as 1664, of the 516 households listed in the hearth tax returns only 244 (around 47 per cent) were eligible to pay the tax. The others were either too impoverished or still living in insubstantial or non-repaired hovels. Rebuilding could only occur as finance became available and, for many citizens, it was decades rather than months before such sums could be recuperated.

Even when the fighting ended there were other factors that continued to disrupt the previously orchestrated life of the town's citizens. With the triumph of Parliament over the king, great upheavals were instigated in the realms of Christian worship and the structure of the church. The familiar landscape of Prayer Book worship, with its cycle of saint days, ceremonial and liturgy, were swept away in the Puritan quest for a less catholic structured church with worship based on simple Biblical models. Up until the surrender of the town in 1646, Newark had managed to avoid such impositions and even as negotiations were underway for the surrender of the garrison parishioners and clergy managed to dismantle or hide away the furniture and equipment of its Anglican worship. *The Prayer Book*, the *Book of Homilies* and even the organ were spirited away in 1646, not to reappear until 1661. This suggests that the town's compliance with Parliamentarian ordinances was never anything more than outward conformity. The Song School was certainly closed down, its Master dismissed and its choir removed from public worship. For the town's parishioners the visible and audible quality of worship was considerably diminished, yet in spite of these token acts of conformity to the new regime there were overt acts of disobedience (such as the keeping of the registers) which testify to the survival of Anglicanism within the town.

The 1650s witnessed a subtle change in the town's ruling elite as former Royalists were barred from holding office. The extent to which their replacements were unable to become established in office throughout the 1650s is clearly demonstrated by the ease with which they were removed at the Restoration of Charles II. Much of the Puritan legislation passed in the 1650s regarding Sabbath observance and the improvement of morals was imposed upon the town, but failed to attract much sympathy or win the hearts of Newark's inhabitants. Newark's Royalist past meant that it was closely monitored and supervised throughout the 1650s and so was unable to do anything other than begrudgingly comply with these impositions.

This research, based on the surviving records of everyday life in Newark over the period, clearly demonstrates that for the ordinary citizens of the town, the impact of the British Civil Wars extended way beyond the end of the actual fighting. Indeed, the economic and demographic consequences were to extend over several decades and well into the eighteenth-century. Unlike the ports of Bristol or Chester, or the growing industrial areas in the Ridings of Yorkshire, trade and commerce were not well enough established in the region to drive forward a swift recovery. The conflict did create, however, a civic and community spirit that was successful in imparting a real sense of identity to its citizens. The numerous visits of Stuart royalty over the years 1641-1646 and the town's brave endurance of three sieges instilled in Newark a lasting sense of patriotism.

End Notes

Introduction

1. E.S. De Beer (ed.), *The Diary of John Evelyn* (Oxford, 1959), p.347
2. Daniel Defoe, *A Tour Through the Whole Island of Great Britain* (London: Penguin, 1971)
3. Royal Commission on Historical Monuments (hereafter RCHM), *Newark on Trent: The Civil War Siegeworks* (1964)
4. For a published copy of the latter see M. Bennett, S. Jennings and M. Whyld, 'Two Military Account Books for the Civil War in Nottinghamshire', *Transactions of the Thoroton Society (hereafter TTS)*, 100 (1996)
5. A. C. Wood, *Nottinghamshire in the Civil War* (Oxford, 1937) and RCHM, *Newark on Trent*
6. See especially Ronald Hutton, *The British Republic, 1649-1660* (2000)

Chapter 1

7. Christopher Morris (ed.), *The Illustrated Journeys of Celia Fiennes, 1685-c.1712* (Stroud, 1995), pp.84-86
8. Cornelius Brown, *The Annals of Newark-Upon-Trent* (1879), pp.83-84
9. 1 Patent Roll, 2 James I. Part 9
10. See Chapter 2
11. Calendar of State Papers Domestic (hereafter CSPD), 1653-1654, p.19
12. M. W. Barley, 'Newark in the Sixteenth Century', *TTS*, 53 (1949), p.15
13. Trevor Dann and Keith Train, *The Fosse Way* (BBC Radio Nottingham, 1976), pp.31-31
14. Stuart B. Jennings, "'The Gathering of the Elect': The Development, Nature and Social-Economic Structures of Protestant Religious Dissent in Seventeenth Century Nottinghamshire" (Unpublished Ph.D. Thesis, Nottingham Trent University, 1999), Chapter 1
15. Barley, 'Newark in the Sixteenth Century', pp.16-17
16. R. F. B. Hodgkinson (ed.), *Extracts from the Records of the Borough of Newark-Upon-Trent* (Newark, 1921), p.21
17. Barley, 'Newark in the Sixteenth Century', p.22
18. Brown, *Annals of Newark-Upon-Trent*, p.81
19. Morris, *Illustrated Journeys of Celia Fiennes*, pp.84-86
20. Hodgkinson, *Extracts from the Records of the Borough*, p.38
21. Hodgkinson, *Extracts from the Records of the Borough*, pp.17-18
22. Most of this paragraph is derived from Pamela Marshall and John Samuels, *Guardian of the Trent; The Story of Newark Castle* (Nottinghamshire County Council, 1997)
23. Brenda M. Pask, *Newark Parish Church of St. Mary Magdalene* (Newark, 2000), pp.28-30
24. Keith Train, *Train on Churches* (BBC Radio Nottingham, 1981) Article on Newark Church
25. Pask, *Newark Parish Church*, p.66
26. R. F. B. Hodgkinson, *Extracts from Newark Churchwarden Accounts* (Newark, 1922), p.15
27. Malcolm Fox, 'Urban Elite and Town Government: Newark-on-Trent in the Mid Seventeenth Century (Unpublished MA Thesis, University of Nottingham, 1985), pp.3-4
28. Hodgkinson, *Extracts from the Records of the Borough*, p.9
29. Ibid., p.8
30. Nottinghamshire Archives (hereafter NA), DC/NW/3/1/1, Newark Borough Corporation Minutes (hereafter Borough Minutes), entries for 3 January 1636 and 27 March 1640
31. Hodgkinson, *Extracts from the Records of the Borough*, p8
32. Fox, 'Urban Elite and Town Government', p.6
33. Hodgkinson, *Extracts from the Records of the Borough*, p.10
34. A. C. Wood, *Nottinghamshire in the Civil War* (2nd edn., Wakefield, 1971), p.6
35. A. C. Wood, 'A Note on the Population of Six Nottinghamshire Towns in the 17th Century', *TTS*, 41 (1937) and W. F. Webster (ed.), *Nottinghamshire Hearth Tax, 1664: 1674* (Thoroton Society Record Series, XXXVII, 1988), pp.xxi-xxiii
36. See Chapter 5 for more details
37. M. D. Gordon, 'The Collection of Ship-money in the Reign of Charles I', *Transactions of the Royal Historical Society*, IV (third Series, 1910), pp.141-162

[38] CSPD 1637, 18 September 1637, p.423

[39] CSPD 1637-1638, 24 March 1638, p.326

[40] CSPD 1638-1639, p.151

[41] CSPD 1639, 8 May 1639, p.134

[42] CSPD 1639-1649, 17 February 1640, p.465

[43] CSPD 1637, p.411

[44] NA, Newark Borough Miscellaneous Papers (hereafter Newark Borough Misc.) [DC/NW] D6.75/Bundle C22/1-9

[45] W. G. Hoskins, 'Harvest Fluctuations in English Economic History, 1620-1759', *Agricultural History Review* XVI (1968), pp.15-45

Chapter 2

[46] Wood, *Nottinghamshire in the Civil War*, p.16

[47] William Dickinson, *The History and Antiquities of the Town of Newark in the County of Nottingham* (London, 1819); Cornelius Brown, The History of Newark. 2vols (Newark, 1904); Cornelius Brown, *The Annals of Newark-on-Trent* (London, 1879); Alfred C. Wood, *Nottinghamshire in the Civil War* (Oxford, 1937); RCHM, *Newark-on-Trent*; Tim Warner, *Newark: Civil War & Siegeworks* (Nottinghamshire County Council, 1992); Martyn Bennett, *The Civil wars Experienced: Britain and Ireland, 1638-1661* (London, 2000); Martyn Bennett (ed.), *A Nottinghamshire Village in War and Peace: The Accounts of the Constables of Upton, 1640-1666* (Thoroton Society, Nottingham, 1995)

[48] Brown, *Annals of Newark-on-Trent*, p.114

[49] A. C. Wood, *Memorials of the Holles Family*, Camden Third Series, LV (London, 1937), p.viii

[50] Wood, *Nottinghamshire in the Civil War*, p.24

[51] Martyn Bennett, Stuart Jennings and Martin Whyld, 'Two Military Account Books for the Civil War in Nottinghamshire', TTS, 100 (1996), pp.107-121

[52] Nottinghamshire University Manuscripts Department (hereafter NUMD), The Mellish Papers, Me Lm 11, The Account of John Twentyman

[53] Wood, *Nottinghamshire in the Civil War*, p.29

[54] N. H. Keeble (ed.), Lucy Hutchinson, *Memoirs of the Life of Colonel Hutchinson* (London: Everyman, 1995), pp.94-95

[55] Peter Edwards, 'Logistics and Supplies' in John Kenyon and Jane Ohlmeyer (eds.), *The Civil Wars. A military History of England, Scotland and Ireland, 1638-1660* (Oxford, 1998), pp. 234-271

[56] Calendar for the Advance of Money Causes, 1643-56, 3 Vols. (1888), p.1018

[57] Wood, *Nottinghamshire in the Civil War*, p.44

[58] Wilfrid Emberton, *The English Civil War Day by Day* (Stroud, 1995), p.61

[59] Warner, *Newark: Civil War and Siegeworks*, p.13

[60] Wood, *Nottinghamshire in the Civil War*, p.49

[61] NA, Borough Minutes, 1642-1674, DC/NW/3/1/1

[62] Wood, *Nottinghamshire in the Civil War*, p.73

[63] For another account see British Library, *A Brief Relation of the Siege of Newark (1643)*, E.39

[64] Ibid. p.80

[65] Wood, *Nottinghamshire in the Civil War*, p.94

[66] See Chapter 3

[67] Bennett, Jennings & Whyld, 'Two Military Account Books for Nottinghamshire', pp.116-117

[68] Wood, *Nottinghamshire in the Civil War*, p.92

[69] Philip Aubrey, *Mr Secretary Thurloe, Cromwell's Secretary of State, 1652-1660* (1990), pp.110-112

[70] Glenn Foard, *Naseby, The Decisive Campaign* (Whitstable, 1995), pp.265-267, 320

[71] Wood, *Nottinghamshire in the Civil War*, p.94

[72] NA, Draft Warrant to Sir Richard Willis 22 August 1645, [DC/NW] D48.74/30

[73] See Chapter 3 and also Newark Borough Misc. Hospitality voucher [DC/NW] D6.75/C43/26 and Soldiers voucher D6.75/C22/13

Chapter 3

[74] See Bennett, Jennings & Whyld, 'Two Military Account Books for Nottinghamshire', pp.107-121

[75] Martyn Bennett, 'Contribution and Assessment: Financial Extractions in the English Civil War, 1642-1646', *War and Society*, 4 (May, 1986), p.2

[76] NA, Thorpe-by-Newark Constable's Accounts, PR/5,767

[77] Bennett, 'Contribution and Assessment', p.6

[78] See Ian Gentles, 'The Civil Wars in England' in John Kenyon and Jane Ohlmeyer (eds.), *The Civil Wars. A Military History of England, Scotland and Ireland, 1638-1660* (Oxford, 19998), p.106 and John Kenyon, *The Civil Wars of England* (1988), pp.125-126

[79] Cornelius Brown, *A History of Newark-on-Trent*, 2 vols. (Newark, 1907), II, pp.84-85

[80] R. F. B. Hodgkinson, *Extracts from the Records of the Borough of Newark-upon-Trent* (Newark, 1921), p.40

[81] NA, [DC/NW] D48.74/32, 29 December 1647

[82] CSPD, 1661-1662, and Cornelius Brown, *The Annals of Newark-upon-Trent* (1879), p.187

[83] C. H. Firth, *Cromwell's Army: A History of the English Soldier during the Civil Wars, the Commonwealth and the Protectorate* (University Paperbacks, 1962), pp.216-218

[84] NA, Newark Churchwarden Accounts 1643(4), PR/24,810 (hereafter Churchwarden Accounts)

[85] NA, Borough Minutes, DC/NW/3/1/1, 16 December 1650

[86] Martin Bennett (ed.), *A Nottinghamshire Village in War and Peace: The Accounts of the Constables of Upton, 1640-1660* (Thoroton Society Record Series: Nottingham, 1995)

[87] Bennett, *Upton Constable Accounts*, p.22

[88] Ibid., p.14

[89] Ibid., p.26

[90] Ibid., pp. 28, 31, 34

[91] Ibid., p.27

[92] John Kenyon, *The Civil Wars of England*, pp.128-129

[93] Bennett, *Upton Constable Accounts*, p.32

[94] Brown, *History of Newark*, II, p.65

[95] NA, Borough Minutes, DC/NW/3/1/1, March 1644

[96] In fact 10 of then did not even appear on the initial list of 1649

[97] NA Newark Borough Misc. Chamberlains Accounts, 1644 [DC/NW] D6.75/C28/8

[98] The following paragraphs are derived from Bennett, Jennings and Whyld, 'Two Military Account Books for Nottinghamshire', pp.107-121

[99] Ibid., pp.118-119

[100] NA, Newark Borough Misc. [DC/NW] D6.75/C28/8 and Churchwarden Accounts, PR/24,810

[101] Brown, *History of Newark*, II, pp.121-122

[102] Bennett, *Upton Constable Accounts*, p.11

[103] NA, Newark Borough Misc.Vouchers [DC/NW] D6.75/C46/7 and D6.75/C43

[104] NA, Newark Borough Misc. [DC/NW] D6.75/C1/68

[105] NA, Newark Borough Misc. [DC/NW] D6.75/C1/67

[106] NA, Newark Borough Misc. [DC/NW] D6.75/C22/1

[107] Calendar of the Committee for Compounding with Delinquents, 1643-1660 (hereafter CCC), II, p.1319

[108] RCHM, *Newark on Trent*, p.82

[109] The loose notes are inserted into a printed volume from the Mellish Papers. NA, Me Lm 11

[110] CCC, II, p.1348 and III, p.1743 Also see Calendar of the Proceedings of the Committee for Advancement of Money Causes (hereafter CAMC), p.1011

[111] CCC, I, p.535 and II, p.1419

[112] NA, Newark Borough Misc. Chamberlain's Accounts 1644-1645, [DC/NW] D6.75/C28/8

[113] Ian Gentles, 'The Civil Wars in England', p.106

[114] Richard Franck, *Northern Memoirs* (Edinburgh, 1821), pp.269-270

[115] British Library, A Continuation of True Intelligence from the Army under the Command of the Earl of Manchester, from July 27th to August 16th 1644 (London, Wood Street, 1644)

[116] Bennett, *Upton Constable Accounts*, p.32

[117] Ibid., p.34

[118] Brown, *History of Newark*, II, p.85

[119] Diary of Abraham de la Pryme, *Surtees Society*, 54, pp.108-110. Entry for 13 August 1695

[120] Brown, *History of Newark*, II, pp.125-126

[121] Calendar of Committee for Advancement of Money Causes (1888), II, p.1073

[122] NA, Newark Borough Misc. [DC/NW] D6.75/23/26

[123] NA, Newark Borough Misc. Chamberlain's Accounts 1644-1645, [DC/NW] D6.75/C28/8

[124] NA, Borough Minutes, DC/NW/3/1/1, May 1646, p.214b

[125] NA, Military Documents D48.74/30

[126] *A Great Fight at Newarke* (London, 10 March 1646)

[127] Brown, *History of Newark*, II, p.119

[128] NA, Newark Borough Misc. Hospitality Voucher [DC/NW] D6.75/C43

[129] Ibid., [DC/NW] D6.75/C22/12

[130] W. G. Hoskins, 'Harvest Fluctuations in English Economic History,1620-1759', *Agricultural History Review*, XVI (1968)

[131] NA, Borough Minutes, DC/NW/3/1/1, 2 December 1647, p.218

[132] Ibid., February 1648(9), p.220

[133] RCHM, *Newark on Trent*, p.29

[134] Barley, 'Newark in the Sixteenth Century', TTS, p.17

[135] NA, Borough Minutes, DC/NW/3/1/1

[136] RCHM, *Newark on Trent*, p.26

[137] NUMD, Twentiman Manuscript, Mexv

[138] Numerous manuals survive, see especially Paul Ive, *The Practice of Fortification* (London, 1589)

[139] R. Thoroton, *The Antiquities of Nottinghamshire* (Nottingham, 1677), pp.197-198

[140] Ibid.

[141] See Chapter 5

[142] NUMD, Twentiman Manuscript, Mexv

[143] NA, Newark Borough Records, Hospitality Vouchers, [DC/NW] D6.75/C43

[144] Stephen Porter, *Destruction in the English Civil Wars* (Stroud, 1994), pp.18-20

[145] Porter, *Destruction in the Civil Wars*, p.47

[146] Newark Library, Will of Hercules Clay dated 11 December 1644. Typed Transcript, L98.3CLA

[147] NA, Will of Thomas Waite, PR/NW 22 October 1645 (petition is on reverse of the will)

[148] Cornelius Brown, *The Annals of Newark (London, 1879)*, p.138

[149] NA, Newark Military Documents, Warrant to Colonel Frescheville, D48.74/29

[150] NA, Churchwarden Accounts

[151] NA, Churchwarden Accounts, 17 April 1645

[152] NA, Newark Borough Misc, Market Cross Voucher [DC/NW] D6.75/C46

[153] NA, Borough Minutes, DC/NW/3/1/1, p.214a

[154] quoted in Cornelius Brown, *A History of Newark-on-Trent*, II, p.106

[155] Ibid. p.104

[156] British Library, *Mercurius Civicus, London Intelligencer, Thursday April 16th – Thursday April 23rd, 1646* (London, 1646)

[157] British Library, Thomason Tract, E 506 (35) *A Perfect Diurnall of Some Passages in Parliament, 20-27 April 1646*, p.1144 and E 509 (1), *A Perfect Diurnall....27 April – 4 May 1646*, p.1158

[158] See especially Chapter 7

[159] CSPD, 1661-1662, p.45, 27 July 1661

[160] W. T. Webster (ed.), *Nottinghamshire Hearth Tax, 1664: 1674* (Thoroton Society Record Series, 1988)

[161] Quoted in Porter, *Destruction in the Civil Wars*, p.97

[162] Ibid., pp.97-98

Chapter 4

[163] Andrew Cunningham and Ole Peter Grell, *The Four Horsemen of the Apocalypse: Religion, War, Famine and Death in Reformation Europe* (Cambridge, 2000), pp.270-272

[164] John Adair, By the Sword Divided: *Eyewitnesses of the English Civil War* (London, 1983), p.79

165 Glenn Foard, *Naseby, the Decisive Campaign* (Whitstable, 1995), pp.317-318 and J. A. Dils, 'Epidemics, Mortality and the Civil War in Berkshire, 1642-46' in R. C. Richardson, *The English Civil Wars, Local Aspects*

166 Wood, *Nottinghamshire in the Civil War*, p.6

167 W. F. Webster, ed. *Nottinghamshire Hearth Tax, 1664: 1674* (Thoroton Society record Series, 1988), p.xxiii

168 Wood, *Nottinghamshire in the Civil War*, p.30

169 Warner, *Newark: Civil War and Siegeworks*, p.13

170 Bennett, Jennings & Whyld, 'Two military Account Books for Nottinghamshire', pp.118-119

171 For a fuller discussion of this see Chapter 3

172 Andrew Appleby, *Famine in Tudor and Stuart England* (Stanford University Press: California, 1978), pp.102-105

173 NA, Newark Parish Registers, 1629-1649 PR27,256 and PR27,257

174 Wood, *Nottinghamshire in the Civil War*, p.89

175 See Chapter 2

176 Appleby, *Famine in Tudor and Stuart England*, pp.99-101

177 NA, Newark Military Documents. D48.74/30 Draft Warrant authorising the bringing into the town of corn from the surrounding countryside.

178 NA, Newark Borough Misc. Visit House Vouchers [DC/NW] D6.75/C46/3-9

179 NA, Newark Borough Misc. [DC/NW] D6.75/C46/7   A different hand has dated this bill December 1646 but Gonison was churchwarden only up until March 1646 and he died of plague in June 1646.

180 NA, Newark Borough Misc. [DC/NW] D6.75/C46/4

181 NUMD, Twentiman Manuscript, Mexv

182 Wood, *Nottinghamshire in the Civil War*, p.98

183 John Lynch, *For King and Parliament, Bristol and the Civil War* (Stroud, 1999), p.163

184 Wood, *Nottinghamshire in the Civil War*, pp.108-110

185 NA, Borough Minutes, 1642-1674, DC/NW/3/1/1 279v-280

186 NA, Will of Christopher Richards PR/NW 20 November 1646 & Will of William Barrett PR/NW 20 November 1646

187 NA, Borough Minutes, DC/NW/3/1/1 p.215b

188 NA, Churchwarden's Accounts PR/24,810, 1643-1644

189 NA, Newark Borough Misc. [DC/NW] D6.75/C46/4   A different hand has added the date Christmas 1645 to the reverse of the original bill.

190 Most of this paragraph is derived from Paul Slack, *The Impact of Plague in Tudor and Stuart England* (Oxford, 1995), pp.26-32

191 NA, Newark Borough Misc. [DC/NW] D6.75/C46/9

192 Cornelius Brown, *A History of Newark-on-Trent* (Newark, 1907), 2 vols. II, p.102

193 CSPD, 1645-46, p.356

194 T. Bailey, *Annals of Nottinghamshire: History of the County of Nottingham including the Borough* (4 vols., Nottingham, 1853), II, p.763

195 Wood, *Nottinghamshire in the Civil War*, p.107

196 N. H. Keeble (ed.), Lucy Hutchinson, *Memoirs of the Life of Colonel Hutchinson with a Fragment of Autobiography* (1995), p.206

197 Martyn Bennett, *A Nottinghamshire Village in War and Peace, The Accounts of the Constables of Upton, 1640-1666*, Thoroton Society Record Series, XXXIX (1995), p.40

198 NA, Will of Robert Gonison, PR/NW 27 April 1647

199 RCHM, *Newark on Trent*, pp.92-93

200 CSPD, 1645-47, p.552

201 NA, Farndon Parish Register, PR/21,774

202 Brown, *A History of Newark on Trent*, II, p.120

203 NA, East Stoke Parish Register, PR/346

204 NA, Will Of Robert Baguley of East Stoke PR/NW 18 March 1647

205 Bennett, *A Nottinghamshire Village in War and Peace*, p.42

206 NA, Thorpe-by-Newark Account Book, PR/5,767

207 Peter Wenham, *The Great and Close siege of York, 1644* (York, 1994), pp.132-139

208 Brown, *A History of Newark-on-Trent*, II, p.133

209 Paul Slack, 'The Local Incidence of Epidemic Disease: The Case of Bristol, 1540-1650' in *The Plague Reconsidered* (Local Population Studies Supplement, 1977), pp.49-62

Chapter 5

210 David Cressy, *Birth, Marriage and Death: Ritual, Religion and the Life-cycle in Tudor and Stuart England* (OUP, 1999), p.285

211 Cressy, *Birth, Marriage and Death*, p.298

212 Details extracted from NA, Newark Church Registers PR/27,257

213 Ibid.

214 See Chapter 6

215 NA, Newark Borough Misc. [DC/NW] D6.75/C4/17

216 NA, Newark Borough Misc. [DC/NW] D6.75/C4/18

217 NA, Newark Borough Misc. [DC/NW] D6.75/C39/5

218 Calendar of the Proceedings of the Committee for Advancement of Money Causes, p.1011

219 M. Bennett (ed.), *A Nottinghamshire Village in War and Peace, The Accounts of the Constables of Upton, 1640-1666* (Thoroton Society Record Series, XXXIX, 1995), p.35

220 Bennett, *Upton Constable Accounts*, pp.28, 32

221 Bennett, *Upton Constable Accounts*, p.31

222 NA, Newark Borough Misc. [DC/NW] D6.75/C16/14

223 NA, Borough Minutes, DC/NW/3/1/1, p.215b

224 NA, Newark Borough Misc. [DC/NW] D6.75/H6/2

225 NA, Newark Borough Misc. [DC/NW] D6.75/C21/21-27

226 NA, Churchwarden Accounts PR/24,810, 1646

227 NA, Newark Borough Misc. [DC/NW] D6.75/C32/9-10

228 N. G. Jackson, *Newark Magnus, The Story of a Gift* (Nottingham, 1964), p.59

229 NA, Newark Borough Misc. [DC/NW] D6.75/C23/26

Chapter 6

230 S. R. Gardiner, *The Constitutional Documents of the Puritan Revolution, 1625-1660* (Oxford, reprint 1968), p.388, An Act Declaring England to be a Commonwealth

231 H. Hampton Copnall, *Notes and Extracts from the Nottinghamshire County Records of the 17th century* (Nottingham, 1915), p.85

232 Fox, 'Newark on Trent', p.10

233 C. H. Firth & R. S. Rait (eds.), *Acts and Ordinances of the Interregnum* (1911), 2 vols., I. p.1023 and II. P.241

234 NA, Borough Minutes, 1642-1664, DC/NW/3/1/1, p.222 September 1650

235 Cornelius Brown, *The Annals of Newark-Upon-Trent* (1879), p.331

236 See especially Philip Styles, 'The City of Worcester during the Civil Wars, 1640-1660', in R. C. Richardson (ed.), *The English Civil Wars; Local Aspects* (Stroud, 1997), pp.187-238

237 NA, Will of Matthew Newham, PR/NW 14 February 1685

238 Derived from data provided in Fox, 'Newark on Trent', p.69

239 Fox, 'Newark on Trent', p.43

240 NA, Borough Minutes, DC/NW/3/1/1, pp.238-238a

241 Fox, 'Newark on Trent', p.53

242 NA, Newark Borough Misc. [DC/NW] D6.75/H33/3/10

243 NA, Borough Minutes, DC/NW/3/1/1, p.233

244 Ibid, p.233b

245 Ibid, pp.226b, 240b

246 NA, Nottinghamshire Quarter Session Minutes C/QS/M/1/13, 10 January 1655

247 Fox, 'Newark on Trent', p.58

248 Wood, *Nottinghamshire in the Civil War*, p.174

249 Ronald Hutton, *The Restoration: A Political and Religious History of England and Wales, 1658-1667* (Oxford, 1985), pp.21-22

250 Copnall, *Notes and Extracts*, p.96

[251] W. G. Hoskins, 'Harvest Fluctuations in English Economic History, 1620-1759', *Agricultural History Review* XVI (1968), pp.15-45

[252] G. E. Aylmer & J. S. Morrill, *The Civil War and Interregnum: Sources for Local Historians* (London, 1979), pp.13-14

[253] Fox, 'Newark on Trent', p.47

Chapter 7

[254] 'To the greater glory of God'

[255] NA, Churchwardens Accounts, PR/24,810, 1642

[256] R. F. B. Hodgkinson, *Newark Churchwarden Accounts* (Newark, 1921), pp. 6-8

[257] Henry Thorold, *A Shell Guide: Nottinghamshire* (London, 1984), pp.109-115 and Brenda M. Pask, *The Parish Church of St. Mary Magdalene, Newark-on-Trent, Nottinghamshire* (Newark District Council, 1995)

[258] R. A. Marchant, 'The Restoration of Nottinghamshire Churches, 1635-1640', TTS, 65 (1961), pp.77-80

[259] Brenda M. Pask, *Newark Parish Church of St. Mary Magdalene* (Newark, 2000), p.77

[260] All the following details are taken from the Newark Churchwarden Accounts, NA, PR 24,810

[261] Martyn Bennett, *The English Civil War: A Historical Companion* (Stroud, 2004), p.77

[262] C. E. Long (ed.), *Richard Symonds's Diary of the Marches of the Royal Army* (Cambridge, 1997), p.229

[263] Wood, *Nottinghamshire in the Civil War*, p.225

[264] NA, Newark Borough Misc. [DC/NW] D6.75/C22/3, D6.75/C43 and D6.75/C22/4

[265] NA, C/QS/M/1/12, p.256

[266] NA, Borough Minutes, DC/NW/3/1/1, p.223b

[267] J. P. Kenyon, *The Stuart Constitution* (Oxford, 1986), pp.312-315

[268] Stuart B Jennings, 'The Gathering of the Elect: The Development, Nature and Social-Economic Structures of Protestant Religious Dissent in Seventeenth Century Nottinghamshire', (Unpublished Ph.D. Thesis, Nottingham Trent University, 1999), p.165

[269] Stuart Jennings, 'The 1669 Ecclesiastical Returns for Nottinghamshire: A Reassessment of the Strength of Protestant Nonconformity', *Transactions of the Thoroton Society*, XCIX (1995), pp.73-80

[270] J. P. Kenyon, *The Stuart Constitution* (Cambridge, 1986), p.242

[271] Guy de la Bédoyére (ed.), *The Diary of John Evelyn* (1995), p.86

[272] Ronald Hutton, *The Restoration: A Political and Religious History of England and Wales, 1658-1667* (Oxford, 1985), Chapters 1-4

[273] NA, Churchwarden's Accounts, PR/24,810, 1661

[274] Inscription on the restored font in St. Mary Magdalene Parish Church, Newark.

[275] Keith Train, *Train on Churches* (BBC Radio Nottingham Publication, 1981)

[276] Robert Latham (ed.), *The Shorter Pepys* (1986), p.101

[277] David Cressy, *Bonfires and Bells* (Stroud, 2004), pp.18-19

[278] John Morrill, 'The Impact of Puritanism' in John Morrill (ed.), *The Impact of the English Civil War* (London, 1991), pp.50-66

[279] Jennings, '1669 Ecclesiastical Returns', pp.73-80

BIBLIOGRAPHY

PRIMARY MANUSCRIPT SOURCES ARRANGED
BY REPOSITORIES

NOTTINGHAMSHIRE ARCHIVES

C/QS/M/1/11, 12, 13	Nottinghamshire Quarter Session Minutes, 1640-1660
DC/NW/3/1/1	Newark Borough Council Minutes, 1640-1660
[DC/NW] D6.75	Newark Borough Council Miscellaneous Papers, 1600-1662 (uncatalogued Newark Museum collection)
D48.74	Newark Military Documents, 1642-1648 (uncatalogued Newark Museum collection, originally held by Gilstrap Library)
PR/NW	Newark Wills, 1640-1660 (Filed by date proven)
PR/24,810	Newark Churchwarden Accounts 1640-1662
PR/27,256-27,257	Newark Parish Registers, 1640-1660
PR/346	East Stoke Parish Register
PR/21,774	Farndon Parish Register
PR/5,767	Thorpe by Newark Account Book of Parish Officers including Constables' Accounts
PR/1,710	Upton Constables' Accounts, 1640-1666
PR/1,531	Coddington Constables' Accounts, 1641-1769
PR/1549	Coddington Town Levies, 1639-1703

NOTTINGHAM UNIVERSITY MANUSCRIPTS DEPARTMENT

A11-A60	Archdeaconry of Nottingham Act Books
PB328, 329	Newark Deanery Seventeenth Century Presentment Bills
Me Lm 11	The Mellish Papers; Twentyman Manuscript

THE NATIONAL ARCHIVES

SP 28/174	Commonwealth Exchequer papers, Sequestration Accounts
SP 29/68 19	A List of Officers Claiming to the Sixty thousand Pounds etc. Granted by His Sacred Majesty for the relief of his truly loyal and Indigent Party.

PRINTED PRIMARY SOURCES

A Brief relation of the Siege of Newark (1644)

A Letter to the Honourable William Lenthal Esq; From the Commissioners Imployed by the Parliament for the reducing of Newark (1646)

Articles Concerning the Surrender of Newark (1646)

Barley, M. W., *Documents Relating to the manor and Soke of Newark-on-Trent*, Thoroton Record Series, XVI (Nottingham, 1956)

Bennett, Martyn (ed.), *A Nottinghamshire Village in War and Peace: The Accounts of the Constables of Upton, 1640-1660*, Thoroton Society Record Series, XXXIX (Nottingham, 1995)

Calendar of State Papers Domestic, Charles I (1891)

Calendar of the Committee for Compounding with Delinquents, 1643-1660 (1880)

Calendar of the Proceedings of the Committee for Advancement of Money Causes (1888)

Firth, C. H. (ed.), *The Journal of Prince Rupert's Marches, 5 Sept 1642 to 4 July 1646*, English Historical Review, XIII (1898)

Hodgkinson, R. F. B., *Extracts from the Records of the Borough of Newark-Upon-Trent* (Newark, 1921)

Hodgkinson, R. F. B., *Newark Churchwardens' Accounts* (Newark, 1922)

My Lord Newark's Speech to the trained-bands of Nottinghamshire at Newark, 13. July 1642 (1642)

Webster, W. F. (ed.), *Nottinghamshire Hearth Tax 1664: 1674*, Thoroton Society Record series, XXXVII (Nottingham, 1988)

SECONDARY SOURCES

BOOKS

Adair, John, *By the Sword Divided: Eyewitnesses of the English Civil War* (1983)

Appleby, Andrew, A., *Famine in Tudor and Stuart England* Stanford, California, 1978)

Ashley, Maurice, *The English Civil War* (1990)

Atkin, Malcolm, *Worcestershire under Arms. An English County during the Civil Wars* (Barnsley, 2004)

Aylmer, G. E., *The Interregnum: The Quest for Settlement* (1972)

Aylmer, G. E. and Morrill, John, *The Civil War and Interregnum: Sources for Local Historians* (1979)

Bailey, T., *Annals of Nottinghamshire* (1853)

Barnard, Toby, *The English Republic, 1649-1660* (1990)

Barratt, John, *Cavaliers: The Royalist Army at War, 1642-1646* (Stroud, 2000)

Barratt, John, *The Great Siege of Chester* (Stroud, 2003)

Bennett, Martyn (ed.), *Society, Religion and Culture in Seventeenth-century Nottinghamshire* (Lampeter, 2005)

Bennett, Martyn, *The Civil Wars Experienced* (2000)

Bennett, Martyn, *The Civil Wars in Britain and Ireland, 1638-1651* (Oxford, 1997)

Bennett, Martyn, *The English Civil Wars: A Historical Companion* (Stroud, 2004)

Brown, Cornelius, *History of Newark*, 2 vols. (Newark, 1904)

Brown, Cornelius, *The Annals of Newark-Upon-Trent* (1879)

Carlton, Charles, *Going to the Wars, The Experience of the English Civil Wars, 1638-1651* (1992)

Carter, C. Sydney, *The English Church in the Seventeenth Century* (1909)

Cooke, David, *The Civil War in Yorkshire. Fairfax Verses Newcastle* (Barnsley, 2004)

Copnall, H. Hampton, *Notes and Extracts from the Nottinghamshire County records of the 17th Century* (Nottingham, 1915)

Coward, Barry, *Stuart England, 1603-1714* (1997)

Coward, Barry, *The Stuart Age* (1980)

Cressy, David, *Bells and Bonfires* (Stroud, 2004)

Cust, Richard, *Charles I. A Political Life* (2005)

Davies, Godfrey, *The Early Stuarts* (Oxford, 1959)

Dickinson, William, *The History and Antiquities of the Town of Newark in the County of Nottingham* (Newark, 1816)

Durston, Christopher, *Cromwell's Major-generals. Godly Government during the English Revolution* (Manchester University Press, 2001)

Edwards, K. C. (ed.), *Nottingham and its Region* (Nottingham, 1966)

Edwards, Graham, *The Last Days of Charles I* (Stroud, 1999)

Everritt, Alan, *Changes in the Provinces: The Seventeenth Century* (Leicester University Press, 1972)

Everritt, Alan, *The Community of Kent and the Great Rebellion, 1640-1660* (Leicester University Press, 1973)

Everritt, A., *The Local Community and the Great Rebellion* (Historical Association, 1969)

Fincham, Kenneth (ed.), *The Early Stuart Church, 1603-1642* (1993)

Firth, Charles (ed.), *Memoirs of the Life of Colonel Hutchinson, Governor of Nottingham by his Widow Lucy* (1906)

Firth, J. B., *Highways and Byways in Nottinghamshire* (1924)

Foster, Andrew, *The Church of England, 1570-1640* (1994)

Gardiner, S. R., *History of the Great Civil War, 1642-1649*, 4vols. (Moreton-in-the Marsh, 1987)

Gardiner, S. R., *The Constitutional Documents of the Puritan Revolution, 1625-1660* (Oxford, 1906)

Gardiner, S. R., *The First Two Stuarts and the Puritan Revolution* (1876)

Gaunt, Peter, *The British Wars, 1637-1651* (1997)

Gaunt, Peter, *The English Civil Wars, 1642-1651* (Oxford: Osprey, 2003)

Harrington, Peter, *English Civil War Archaeology* (2004)

Harrington, Peter, *English Civil War Fortifications, 1642-1651* (Oxford: Osprey Publishing, 2003)

Harris, Tim, *Restoration. Charles II and his Kingdoms* (2005)

Hey, David, G., *An English Rural Community, Myddle Under the Tudors and Stuarts* (Leicester, 1974)

Hill, Christopher, *Change and Continuity in 17th-Century England* (1994)

Hill, Christopher, *The Century of Revolutions, 1603-1714* (1980)

Hirst, Derek, *England in Conflict, 1603-1660* (1999)

Holmes, C., *Seventeenth Century Lincolnshire* (Lincoln, 1980)

Hughes, Ann, *The Causes of the English Civil War* (1991)

Hunt, Tristram, *The English Civil War at First Hand* (2002)

Hutton, Ronald, *The British Republic* (1990)

Hutton, Ronald, *The Royalist War Effort, 1642-1646* (Second Edition, 1999)

Hutton, Ronald, *The Restoration: A Political and Religious History of England and Wales, 1658-1667* (Oxford, 1985)

Jackson, N. G., *Newark Magnus: The Story of a Gift* (Nottingham, 1964)

Jennings, Stuart, 'When Women preach and Cobblers Pray: The Religious experience of Nottinghamshire, 1640-1662' in Bennett, Martyn (ed), Society, *Religion and Culture in Seventeenth-Century Nottinghamshire* (Lampeter, 2005)

Keeble, N. H., *Lucy Hutchinson, Memoirs of the Life of Colonel Hutchinson* (1995)

Kenyon, John, *The Civil Wars of England* (1988)

Kenyon, John and Ohlmeyer, *The Civil Wars: A Military History of England, Scotland and Ireland, 1638-1660* (Oxford, 1998)

Kenyon, J. P., *The Stuart Constitution, Documents and Commentary* (Cambridge, 1966)

Kishlansky, Mark, *A Monarchy Transformed: Britain, 1603-1714* (1996)

Laslett, Peter, *The World We Have Lost Further Explored* (2000)

Lockyer, Roger, *The Early Stuarts: A Political History of England, 1603-1642* (1989)

Long, C. E., *Richard Symonds's Diary of the Marches of the Royal Army* (Cambridge University Reprint, 1997)

Maltby, Judith, *Prayer Book and People in Elizabethan and Early Stuart England* (Cambridge, 1998)

Marshall, Pamela and Samuels, John, *Guardian of the Trent: The Story of Newark Castle* (Nottinghamshire County Council, 1997)

Morrill, John, *Revolt in the Provinces: The People of England and the Tragedies of War, 1630-1648* (1999)

Morrill, John (ed.), *Revolution and Restoration: England in the 1650s* (1992)

Morrill, John (ed.), *The Impact of the English Civil War* (1991)

Morrill, John, *The Nature of the English Revolution* (1993)

Morris, Christopher (ed.), *The Illustrated Journeys of Celia Fiennes, 1685-c1712* (1982)

Newman, Peter, *Companion to the English Civil Wars* (Oxford, 1990)

Newman, P. R., *Royalist Officers in England and Wales, 1642-1660* (New York, 1981)

O'Day, Rosemary and Heal, Felicity (eds.), *Princes and Paupers in the English Church, 1500-1800* (New Jersey, 1981)

Page, William (ed.), *Victoria County History of Nottinghamshire*, 2 vols. (1910)

Polkey, Andrew, *Civil War in the Trent Valley* (Derby, 1992)

Porter, Stephen, *Destruction in the English Civil Wars* (Stroud, 1994)

Reay, Barry, *Popular Cultures in England, 1550-1750* (1998)

Richardson, R. C., *The English Civil Wars: Local Aspects* (Stroud, 1997)

Roots, Ivan, *The Great Rebellion, 1640-1660* (1966)

Royal Commission on Historical Monuments, *Newark on Trent: The Civil War Siegeworks* (1964)

Royle, Trevor, *Civil War. The Wars of the Three Kingdoms, 1638-1660* (2004)

Russell, Conrad, *The Causes of the English Civil War* (Oxford, 1990)

Scott, David, *Politics and War in the Three Stuart Kingdoms, 1637-1649* (2004)

Sharpe, J. A., *Early Modern England: A Social History, 1550-1760* (Second Edition, 1997)

Sharpe, Kevin, *The Personal Rule of Charles I* (1992)

Sherwood, R. E., *Civil Strife in the Midlands, 1642-1651* (1974)

Shilton, R. P., *The History of the Town of Newark Upon Trent, in the County of Nottingham* (Newark, 1820)

Slack, Paul, *The Impact of Plague in Tudor and Stuart England* (Oxford, 1985)

Slack, Paul, *Poverty and Policy in Tudor and Stuart* (1988)

Steel, Graham, E., *Regicide and Republic: England, 1603-1660* (Cambridge, 2001)

Stone, Lawrence, *The causes of the English revolution, 1529-1642* (1972)

Stoyle, Mark, *Loyalty and Locality* (Exeter, 1994)

Tate, W. E., *The Parish Chest* (Cambridge, 1983)

Thorold, Henry, *Nottinghamshire: A Shell Guide* (1984)

Throsby, J. (ed.), *Robert Thoroton, The Antiquities of Nottinghamshire* (East Ardsley, 1972)

Train, Keith, *Train on Churches* (BBC Radio Nottingham, 1981)

Trotter, Eleanor, *Seventeenth Century Life in the Parish* (1968)

Underdown, David, *Fire from Heaven: Life in an English Town in the Seventeenth Century* (1992)

Warner, Tim, *Newark: Civil War and Siegeworks* (Nottinghamshire County Council, 1992)

Wenham, Peter, *The Siege of York* (York, 1994)

West, Frank, *Rude Forefathers: Upton by Southwell, 1600-1666* (Newark, 1989)

Wheeler, James, Scott, *The Irish and British Wars, 1637-1654* (2002)

Woolrych, Austin, *Britain in Revolution, 1625-1660* (Oxford, 2002)

Worden, Blair, *Roundhead Reputations. The English Civil Wars and the Passions of Prosperity* (2001)

Wrightson, Keith, *English Society, 1580-1680* (1982)

Wroughton, John, *An Unhappy Civil War. The Experience of Ordinary People in Gloucestershire, Somerset and Wiltshire, 1642-1646* (Bath, 1999)

Wood, A. C., *A History of Nottinghamshire* (East Ardsley, 1971)

Wood, Alfred, *Nottinghamshire in the Civil War* (East Ardsley, 1971)

Young, Peter and Holmes, Richard, *The English Civil War* (1974)

JOURNAL ITEMS

Barley, M. W., 'Newark in the Sixteenth Century', *Transactions of the Thoroton Society*, 53 (1949), pp.15-25

Bennett, Martyn, '"My Plundered Townes, My Houses Devastation": The Civil War and North Midlands Life, 1642-1646', *Midland History* 22 (1997), pp.35-50

Bennett, Martyn, Jennings, Stuart & Whyld, Martin, 'Two Military Account Books for the Civil War in Nottinghamshire', *Transactions of the Thoroton Society*, 101 (1997), pp.107-121

Blagg, T. M., 'Village Types and Their Distribution in the Plain of Nottingham', *Geography* (1935), pp.283-294

Brown, Angela, '"Truth is a thing desired": Propaganda and Nottinghamshire during the English Civil War', *Transactions of the Thoroton Society*, 100 (1996), pp.95-106

Dean, Malcolm, J., 'Civil War Siege Defences, Millgate, Newark', *Transactions of the*

Thoroton Society, 79 (1975), pp.68-70

Drage, Christopher, 'An Excavation of the Royalist Town Ditch at Victoria Street, Newark, Nottinghamshire', *Transactions of the Thoroton Society*, 91 (1987), pp.127-132

Hodgkinson, R. F. B., 'The Town Walls of Newark', *Transactions of the Thoroton Society*, 26 (1922), pp.106-109

Hoskins, W. G., 'Harvest Fluctuations in English Economic History, 1620-1759', *Agricultural History Review*, XVI (1968)

Jennings, Stuart, B., 'The 1669 Ecclesiastical Returns for Nottinghamshire', *Transactions of the Thoroton Society*, XCIX (1995), pp.73-80

Jennings, Stuart, B., '"A Miserable, Stinking, Infected Town": Pestilence, Plague and Death in a Civil War Garrison, Newark, 1640-1649', *Midland History*, XXVIII (2003), pp.51-70

Jennings, Stuart B., 'Colonel Isham Parkyns (1601-1671): Nottinghamshire's Forgotten Royalist', *Transactions of the Thoroton Society*, 104 (2000), pp.65-71

Marchant, R. A., 'The Restoration of Nottinghamshire Churches, 1635-40', *Transactions of the Thoroton Society*, LXV (1961), pp.57-93

Samuels, John, Charles, F. W. B., Henstock, Adrian and Siddall, Philip, '"A Very Old Crassy Howse": The Old White Hart Inn, Newark, Nottinghamshire', *Transactions of the Thoroton Society*, 100 (1996), pp.19-54

Seddon, P. R., 'Major General Edward Whalley and the Government of Nottinghamshire, 1655-1656, *Transactions of the Thoroton Society*, 103 (1999), pp.131-139

UNPUBLISHED THESES

Bennett, Martyn, 'The Royalist War Effort in the North Midlands, 1642-1646' (Unpublished Ph.D Thesis, Loughborough University, 1986)

Fox, Malcolm, 'Urban Elite and town Government: Newark on Trent in the Mid-seventeenth Century' (Unpublished MA Thesis, University of Nottingham, 1985)

Jennings, Stuart B., 'The Gathering of the Elect. The Development, nature and Social-Economic structures of Protestant Religious Dissent in Seventeenth Nottinghamshire' (Unpublished Ph.D Thesis, Nottingham Trent University, 1999)

INDEX

Act of Uniformity (1662), 122, 123
Anglo-Scottish Wars, 16-17
arms, 24, 29, 40, 102, 113
assessments, 38-39, 45-46, 49,52
Averham, 79

Baguley, Robert, 80
Badger, 102
Bailey, Robert, 102
Baker, William, 39, 40, 47, 52, 57, 79, 98, 100
Balderton, 77, 79, 81
Ballard, Thomas, Major General, 22-23
Barebones Parliament, 106
Barrett, William, 40, 43, 78
Bellasis, Lord John, 19, 31-32, 51, 58
Belvoir, 24, 30
Bishop's Wars, 16
blackamore, 49
Book of Common Prayer, 3, 85, 109, 112, 114, 120, 123, 126
Boone, Gilbert, 13
Bradmore, 44
Bristol, 73, 84, 127
Browne, Francis, 41, 100
Bunny, 30
Byron, Sir Richard, 26, 31, 40, 43

Cartwright, Hugh, 40
Cavendish, Colonel Charles, 24-26
Cavendish, William, Earl of Newcastle, 21-22, 24, 26-27, 65
Charles I, 9, 12, 15-16, 18-19, 31-33, 49, 73, 97, 115
Charles II, 31, 60, 100, 112, 119, 121, 122, 127
Chester, 127
Christmas, 119
Clay, Hercules, 14, 39, 40, 56, 57, 69
Coddington Moor, 2, 91
Commissions of Array, 18, 38-39, 45
Committee for Compounding, 79, 84
Cromwell, 114
Cromwell, Oliver, 25-26, 30, 32, 119
Cromwell, Richard, 103, 120
curfews, 101

Defoe, Daniel, 1
Derby, 20
Devon, river, 7, 8, 60
Dewsberry, William, 117
Directory of Worship, 3, 112, 114
Digby, Sir John, Sheriff of Nottingham, 16, 21, 40, 46, 56

East Stoke, 31, 80
Edgehill (1642), 20, 21, 65
Edwinstowe, 38
Essex, Earl of, 30
Evelyn, John, 1, 119

Fairfax, Sir Thomas, 31-32
Farndon, 31, 77, 79
Fiennes, Celia, 8
Fitzwilliam, Francis, 99, 100
Flower, Thomas, 50
font, church, 116, 120, 122
Fosse Way, 2, 6

Gainsborough, 25-26, 29, 30
Gell, Sir John, 20, 21
Gill, Henry, 47
Gonison, Robert, 43, 78
Goring, Lord George, 32
Grantham, 25, 28
Great North Road, 2, 6, 17, 71, 108
Grey, Lord of Groby, 25
gunpowder, 42-43

Hanckes, Thomas, 40, 43, 46, 98, 100
Harrison, Thomas, 102
Hartrop, Sir Edward, 28
harvests, 17, 52, 105
Hastings, Henry, Lord Loughborough, 28, 44
hearth tax returns (1664, 1674), 14, 61, 76-77, 126
Henderson, Sir John, 21-22, 26, 38, 54, 65
Henrietta, Maria, Queen, 1, 11, 12, 25, 45, 65
Hereford, 32
Hobman, Thoms, 79
Holles, Gervase, 19

141

Hull, 23, 26
Hutchinson, George, 21
Hutchinson, Colonel John, 13, 21, 26, 54, 102
Hutchinson, Lucy, 23, 78

Instrument of Government (1653), 117

James I, 6, 9
James, John, 103, 118
Johnson, John, 14, 40, 99, 100

Kelham Bridge, 97
Knight, William, 78

Langdale, Sir Marmaduke, 31, 32, 44
Laud, William, Archbishop of Canterbury, 2, 109-110, 112, 121
Lee, Gervase, 46
Leeds, 22
Leicester, 32
Lenthal, William, Speaker of the House of Commons, 59
Leslie, General David, 33
Lichfield, 77
Lincoln, 6, 18, 20, 26, 29, 88, 112
loans, 40, 43
London, 6, 18, 111, 119, 121, 123
Lostwithiel (1644), 30
Loughborough, 32
Louth, 30

Magnus Rentals, 50, 94
Magnus, Thomas, 9, 10, 14
Manchester, Earl of, 26, 30
Marriage Act (1653), 87
Marston Moor (1644), 29-30, 69
Martin, John, 14, 40, 43, 47, 91, 100
Maslland, John, 102
Meldrum, Sir John, 26-29, 56
Melton Mowbray, 31, 44
Military Bill (1642), 18
Monck, General George, 120
Montrose, Earl of, 31-32
Morton, 44
Muskham Bridge, 27, 29, 97

Naseby (1644), 32, 44, 48, 50, 58
Newark, 1-3, 6-8, 16, 18, 29, 85
    aldermen, 11
    Borough Corporation, 7, 11-12, 93-94
    castle, 9, 41
    charities, 13, 14
    charters, 10, 11, 13, 60
    churchwardens, 81-83, 115-117
    coinage, 50, 61, 92
    constables, 13, 94-95
    destruction of property, 53-61, 126
    garrison, 38-39, 44, 51-52, 74
    geography, 7
    Grammar School, 9, 94
    Guilds, 10, 11, 108
    inns, 7, 44-45, 65
    Manor, 10, 11, 97
    Mayor, 11, 13
    medieval walls, 6, 8, 9, 21, 53, 54
    mills, 7, 10
    new defences, 21, 23-24, 29, 48, 55, 58-59
    night of the great wind, 121
    poor relief, 13, 89-91
    population, 14-15, 48, 63-65, 85-88, 104-105, 111, 115
    removal of Royalist aldermen, 98-101
    sieges, 19, 27-29, 33-34, 43, 51, 56, 59
    Song School, 10, 95, 126
    Spittal (Earl of Exeter's House) 27-28, 54
    St. Mary Magdalene Parish Church, 10, 57-58, 60, 108, 110-124
    surrender of (1646), 3, 33-34, 52, 77, 97
    town regiment, 46-48
Newcastle, 2, 19
New Model Army, 31-32
Norwell, 24, 46
Nottingham, 6, 19, 20, 21, 25, 111

organ (church), 113-114
Oxford, 19, 27, 31

Parliament, 15, 16, 18, 2
Pepys, Samuel, 121

perambulations, 112-113, 118, 121, 123
Philiphaugh (1644), 44
Piggot, Charles, 56-57
Plague, 3, 34, 52, 70-81, 97
Pontefract, 47
Poulden, William, 47
Poyntz, General Sydenham, 77
preaching ministers, 116, 123
Presbyterians, 16
pulpit (church), 112, 114, 120
Puritan, 114, 122, 124, 126

Quakers, 117
Queningborough, John, 79, 98, 100

Republic (1649), 97-106, 116-120
Restoration (1660), 107, 114, 119,
    120-124
Ridley, Nicholas, 121
Robinson, William, 92
Rossiter, Sir Edward, 44
Roughton, Thomas, 75
royal coat of arms, 120
Rupert, Prince, 1, 28-30, 44, 57, 65, 69
    73, 82

Sabbath Observance, 102, 116, 127
Saville, Lady, 23-24
Scarborough, 48-49
Scottish Army, 1, 18, 27, 32, 33, 59, 62
Selston, 30, 44
Shelford Manor, 24
ship money, 2, 14
Shore, John, 94
Shrove Tuesday, 122
Sleaford, 29-30
Slingsby, Sir Henry, 49-50
soldiers
    at Newark, 21-22, 35, 41, 49
    burials 82-83
    quartering, 41-42, 44-45
    relief of maimed, 103
    wages, 17, 38, 41, 44, 48
Solemn League and Covenant, 27, 33, 62
Stamford, 25
Standish, Edward, 40, 43, 46, 47, 98, 100
Star Chamber, 15

Staunton, Colonel William, 19, 30, 37-38,
    44, 65
Symonds, Richard, 113

Thompson, Lancelot, 47, 100
Thoroton, Dr Robert, 10
Thorpe-by-Newark, 38, 45, 81
Thurgarton, 30
Torksey House, 32
trained bands, 16, 18
Treece, Thomas, 47
Trent, river, 2, 6, 7, 8, 17, 60, 63, 71
Trueman (Trewman), Henry, 39, 40, 47
Twentyman, Edward, 20, 46-47
Twentyman, John, 3, 19, 20, 22-24, 26,
    27-28, 29-30, 31, 73
Twentyman, John Senior, 6
Typhus, 3, 66-70, 125

Upton, 41-42, 45, 78, 81, 91, 92

Waite, Thomas, 56, 59
Watson, William, 13, 14, 43, 99
Welbeck, 26, 30, 32, 49
Wells, George, 43, 47, 100
Whalley, Major-General Edward, 103, 119
Willis, Sir Richard, 31-32, 51
Willoughby, Lord of Parnham, 25
Wilson, Christopher, 39, 40, 57, 98, 101
Winceby (1643), 26
Winthorpe, 59
Wiverton, 24
Worcester, 99

York, 2, 17, 18, 19, 27, 30, 59, 82
Yoxall, Richard, 83, 122

Above: 'A Prospect of Newarke from Lincolne Road' by R. Hall, 1676
(From Robert Thoroton, *Antiquities of Nottinghamshire, 1677)*